OUTSTANDING
BLACK SERMONS

Volume 2

OUTSTANDING
BLACK SERMONS

Volume 2

Walter B. Hoard, editor

Judson Press® Valley Forge

OUTSTANDING BLACK SERMONS, VOLUME 2

Copyright © 1979
Judson Press, Valley Forge, PA 19482-0851

Fifth Printing, 1989

Unless otherwise indicated, Bible quotations in this volume are in accordance with *The Holy Bible*, King James Version.

Other versions of the Bible quoted in this book are:

The Revised Standard Version of the Bible, copyrighted 1946, 1952, 1971, 1973 © by the Division of Christian Education of the National Council of the Churches of Christ in the United States of America, and used by permission.

The New Testament in Modern English, Rev. Ed. Copyright © J. B. Phillips 1972. Used by permission of the Macmillan Company and Geoffrey Bles, Ltd.

The Common Bible, Copyright © 1973 by the Division of Christian Education of the National Council of the Churches of Christ in the United States of America.

Library of Congress Cataloging in Publication Data (Revised)
Main entry under title:

Outstanding Black sermons.

Includes bibliographical references.
1. Sermons, American—Afro-American authors.
I. Smith, James Alfred.   II. Hoard, Walter B.
BV4241.5.09   252   76-2084
ISBN 0-8170-0664-8

The name JUDSON PRESS is registered as a trademark in the U.S. Patent Office.
Printed in the U.S.A.

This book
is
dedicated to

My mother, Mary Tandy Hoard, and my late father,
Reverend Dr. Strobridge Elsworth Hoard

"To those who gave me
so much so often, to
receive so little so
often in return."

My appreciation goes to all the preachers who
allowed their sermons to be published, and to
Mary Frances Lee and Allie Mae Porter for
typing this manuscript.

Contents

Introduction

Every preacher likes to believe that he or she is a great one called by the Almighty to an incomparable task. Perhaps he or she is, for God does not count greatness as humans do. Indubitably though, all preachers and preaching are not the same. America's black pulpiteer is different, probably unique.

Rather than to elucidate on the forces that shaped him or her, suffice it to say that he or she *loves* preaching. It is a joy to one's soul. Without reservation, one laughs at one's peer's exhortations critically and sympathetically. If it's shouting time, one shouts with one's brother, or weeps in exhilaration in the experience of the joy of the gospel.

Black preachers enjoy God's Word. The story is told that two preachers staged a contest to see who could shout the congregation the most. The winner shouted this intellectual audience whooping sweet words about soul food: "chitlins, cornbread, black-eyed peas. . . ." It was not what he said, but *how* he said it. The folks loved it.

Whether this story is fact or fable matters little, since the truth is that black preaching is at the center of black worship and opens the door to God.

Black preachers in American life-style have always had a visible, viable, and potent influence on their people and on society in general. Few people have been able to declare them nonexistent. They have been loved, hated, lynched, and even worshiped at times. More than other black leaders preachers have held the destiny of their people in their hands. They could lead them either through the rugged, encompassing wilderness to the Promised Land, or in retreat, away from the Red Sea into Egypt's bondage.

Even the greatest black preachers, like Mordecai Johnson, Vernon Johns, Howard Thurman, and the black Moses, Martin Luther King, Jr., have been open to severe criticism and distrust. Certain blacks were fearful that even these pulpiteers might lead the race in the wrong direction with their eloquence. Today the same is true. Part of that fear stems from an old saying among black church folks about being made to feel good.

> "Honey, did you go to church today?"
> "Yes, and the sermon was good."
> "What did the preacher say?"
> "Honey, I don't know, but it was the way he said it that counts!"

Historically, though, the black preachers have been next to Jesus; they have been subject to all manner of severe criticism. The way they delivered the message is too often placed far above what was said and how it related to the "good life." This practice makes some of the sisters and brothers tremble. Rightly so, for the content of black preaching must be the gospel of liberation, not enslavement in any form or to any degree. Yet, lest it be forgotten, there has always been a relative, viable content essential to the black pulpiteers and their sheep. For example, in retrospect, the emphasis was on "going to heaven," escape from earthly trials and tribulations, finding a balm in Gilead, laying down one's sword and shield to study war no more, and numerous other theological propositions as written indelibly in the spiritual and in the black experience. Often the critic has failed to comprehend the historical perspective and the hand of the Almighty in the message. Often the critic has refused to accept the fact that black folks have had only the hope shouted in the message from this servant of God. Rather than encouraging their folks to sacrifice their lives like the American Indians, without negating or denying the rights of all men to be free and equal, the preachers implored their brother bondsmen to have faith in a God—in spite of all—who is able to deliver the faithful in his own way and time. So the content was faith, hope, and love instead of hatred, death, and revenge. Historically, because of this kind of message, certain black leaders criticized the pulpit. They saw the ministry as a profession for the ignorant, lazy, and immoral.

In fact, when I was called to the ministry, my preacher uncle told me a "joke" about a black man in Alabama soon after the Emancipation who felt called to preach. He said, "One hot day in July, while this man was at work in the fields picking cotton, suddenly he stopped and raised his head toward heaven, and cried out, 'O my Lord, the cotton is so grassy, the work is so hard, and the sun is so hot that I believe I've been called to preach.'" I got the message loud and clear from my uncle, a Virginia Union University intellectual. He beseeched me not to accept the *call* if I could not preach the gospel fully and sincerely, making it relative to the daily problems and struggles of my people. To him there were too many preachers who had nothing to preach and did more harm than good to the souls of people.

With that kind of challenge what could I do but learn more about the gospel army and the spiritual battlefield to which I was called? Soon I knew the ways of the Sweet Whooper, the Prince of Preachers, the Praying Groaner, the Squealer, the Intellectualizer, the Wanger, the Lecturer, and the Singer. Oddly enough I learned to like all of the various styles of preaching. These were variations on the same theme. Each began with the story of the human fall, ran through various trials and tribulations of the Hebrew children, onto the redemption by Christ, and concluded with a fervid picture of Judgment Day and the fate of the sinner. To me, the absolute inquiry was and still is: "Does black preaching help in the liberation of God's children?" If so, then it is valid whether homiletically proper or not.

Lest I be misunderstood, the black preacher is not a member of the Trinity, even though the people depend on his exhortations so much, so frequently, and in so many different ways. To the contrary, this popularity could be dangerous to the preacher's future. To be exact, the black pulpiteer could very well topple his or her own kingdom. That is because the preacher is imitated so very much by the congregation that Sunday school teachers *preach* their lessons; the deacons *preach* their prayers; the choir *preaches* its songs; and the clerk *preaches* her announcements. No wonder the preacher finds it necessary to jump over the pulpit to get attention.

In spite of what higher or lower criticisms follow black orators around, they are living realities and their message and influence are to be regarded seriously. Make no mistake about it, black preaching is historically unique—its beginning, its raison d'être, its purpose, and the role it plays in the lives of a struggling people. If nothing else—and there is more—preaching is God's main contact with the race. Though the black preacher's kingdom is not absolute anymore, it has not crumbled. Perhaps it will stand forever if the preachers keep their commitment to the Maker and his children. Even today, if the preacher's academic qualifications fall short, if his preaching is "supreme" in the eyes of the beholder, he is King. On the other hand, as expressed in most congregations,

> "A preacher can be forgiven of
> any sin by his congregation,
> except failing to preach well."

If there is a black pulpiteer style, and I feel certain there is, then it is unlike that of any other race. Agreed, the primary purpose of all preaching is *proclamation;* yet unlike other styles, black preaching is not always wholly objective and impersonal but subjective and personal. Just as Jesus used parables, allegories, and stories, for the black preacher much of the same is required. To this style is added the personal touch. A good preacher always spends a few minutes telling how he or she got religion and what it has done for him or her.

If the preacher cannot testify, his or her sermon is suspect. If God has done nothing good for the preacher, God's servant, what's he going to do for the folks in the pews? Nothing?

Finally, the black preacher's message is, more often than not, shot through with the social gospel, an imperative contradiction of conservative preaching, but it must be there. No longer can the preacher's emphasis be on heaven and be effective; instead, he or she must enable God's people to live the abundant life here and now. So the social gospel of the black preacher emphatically declares: "If God doesn't do anything else for me, he sent me—the preacher—to tell you how to live, dress, eat, comb your hair, get an education. He sent me to tell you how, when, and where to start businesses, factories, to vote, and to achieve any goal relative to the abundant life . . . In season and out of season."

As the black preacher goes, so goes the race. He or she is the earthly epitome of God. He or she is God's servant who loves to preach! But the real victories come from loving the people to whom he or she must preach.

To summarize, if certain proper mechanics are essential to "good" preaching, then the black preacher might well be in violation of them. But the essential of good preaching is primarily effectuality. Did it help someone know God better? Improve his or her life-style?

Walter B. Hoard

Are You Looking
for Jesus?

L. Venchael Booth

So Christ was once offered to bear the sins of many; and unto them that look for him shall he appear the second time without sin unto salvation (Hebrews 9:28).

Sir, we would see Jesus (John 12:21).

Our world has never witnessed more confused and turbulent times than at the present. There is depression, trouble, and grief everywhere. There is lack of confidence, lack of trust, and lack of security everywhere—and this is no exaggeration of our predicament in which we seem to find ourselves. We are standing at the door of a bright, new glorious era when peace and goodwill shall reign supreme over strife and hatred. We are standing at the door with a sense of

L. Venchael Booth, L.H.D., D.D., is an organizer, pastor, and preacher known among all Baptists. Dr. Booth was one of the major organizers of the Progressive National Baptist Convention and later served as its president.

Presently he is the pastor of the historic Zion Baptist Church, Cincinnati, Ohio.

helplessness because no one seems to have the key to open this door. We seek a knowledge of the future but are fearful of its consequences. In 1972, it was reported that out of 1,750 daily newspapers in the U.S.A., 1,220 printed regular astrological forecasts. An Australian preacher, Canon Maxwell Arrowsmith, remarked: "How perverse is human nature, how 'unprioritized' the human intellect! We'll *listen* to anything except the Word, we'll *follow* anyone except the Lord. And all the time inevitably, the Day of the Lord is approaching." Hear this word from the Book, he adds: "[God] has fixed a day on which he will judge the world in righteousness by a man whom he has appointed, and of this he has given assurance to all men by raising him from the dead" (Acts 17:31, RSV).

In the midst of all the perversity of our age, when it seems that all the satanic forces are let loose in our society, there is a real need to start *looking for Jesus*. None other can meet our deepest needs. Our children are challenging us as never before. Nothing satisfies this generation. We don't like debts, nor do we like to sacrifice. We don't like discipline, but we want good schools. We don't like jails, but we insist on committing crimes. We decry segregation, but we still want to be different. We want to be elected to office, but we want to doubt the elective process. We want a great moving and powerful church, but we don't want to work and pray it down from heaven. Our world is so confused and troubled that it has lost the sacredness of life. Recently in our city we read reports of buses being burned and destroyed by students. Every year school buildings are vandalized to the tune of many millions of dollars. We need to start looking for Jesus. We need *him in our homes*, in the *marketplaces*, and on *our jobs*. We need him in our hearts to control and regulate our lives. Let us raise some significant questions and suggest some possible answers.

I. Are You Looking for Jesus in Your Servitude?

It is difficult for you and for me to consider ourselves in a state of servitude—but that's exactly where we are. Jesus declared:

No man can serve two masters: for either he will hate the one, and love the other; or else he will hold to the one, and despise the other. Ye cannot serve God and mammon (Matthew 6:24).

This puts us squarely in the role of a servant. There are many people who cannot bear the idea of filling a servant's role in the church, but think it quite all right to become enslaved to a secular organization. "Whosoever committeth sin is the servant of sin" (John 8:34). Some of us would not dare miss a special service in our Fraternity but think nothing of *missing Communion or prayer meeting.* There are only two classes in the church: saints and sinners; redeemed and lost; free servants of God or slaves of sin. The Bible teaches us:

Whosoever committeth sin transgresseth also the law: for sin is the transgression of the law (1 John 3:4).

He that committeth sin is of the devil; for the devil sinneth from the beginning. For this purpose the Son of God was manifested, that he might destroy the works of the devil (1 John 3:8).

It is hard for us to admit that we are not free because the *chains* that bind us are *invisible chains.* There is a heaviness of heart within us because of the weight of sin. We shout more *over our troubles* than we do *over our blessings.* Many of us are not free to worship God on Sundays. We cannot give God the full day. It is not the sin of others that keeps us from enjoying God; it is our own sin that keeps our heads bowed down. We need to look for Jesus in our servitude. He alone is able to set us free.

For whatsoever is born of God overcometh the world: and this is the victory that overcometh the world, even our faith (1 John 5:4).

Ye are of God, little children, and have overcome them: because greater is he that is in you, than he that is in the world (1 John 4:4).

II. Are You Looking for Jesus in Your Solitude?

When a man comes face to face with his *condition,* he is likely to *find himself very much alone.* When he comes to his *moment of truth,* he will discover as Jacob did that he cannot keep on running from his wronged brother. Deception must be faced and atoned for (Genesis 32). Like David in a face-to-face encounter with the prophet Nathan, he discovers that he is the man who stands condemned (2 Samuel 12:7). In such a moment, he can either hang himself like Judas or find mercy like Peter. A man can sometimes stand opposition. He can also sometimes stand a real knock-down fight, but the hardest thing for any man to stand is the *gnawing pain of conscience.* The hard mountain for any man to climb is the realization that "My sin is ever before me" (Psalm 51:3, RSV). The greatest loneliness in the world is to discover that one is lost from the presence of God. The agony was great in the Garden of Gethsemane, but Jesus even then was not alone. It was dark, cold, and cruel Calvary that evoked the cry: "My God, my God, why hast thou forsaken me?" When man faces the gravity of solitude, he needs a frame of reference that has power enough to pull him through. Paul knew persecution, sufferings, shipwrecks, imprisonment, and abandonment. His experience led him to give a great message to the church:

> Looking unto Jesus the author and finisher of our faith; who for the joy that was set before him endured the cross, despising the shame, and is set down at the right hand of the throne of God (Hebrews 12:2).

> For ye know the grace of our Lord Jesus Christ, that, though he was rich, yet for your sakes he became poor, that ye through his poverty might be rich (2 Corinthians 8:9).

In a world like this when the *affections of men vacillate from hot to cold;* when loud proclamations turn out to be mere sounding gongs and tinkling cymbals; when the love of many has waxed cold—there is need for man to look for one who can set his feet upon a rock and establish his goings. That solid rock is Jesus and he is the same today, yesterday, and forever.

III. Are You Looking for Jesus in Your Gratitude?

> Behold, I was shapen in iniquity; and in sin did my mother conceive me (Psalm 51:5).

What we are saying here is not a play on words: Servitude, Solitude, and Gratitude. There is a place for each climate or state in the life of man. He is born in Servitude; he develops and discovers Solitude. When he has been redeemed, he comes forth with Gratitude.

> Bless the Lord, O my soul, and all that is within me, bless his holy name (Psalm 103:1).

Not all men are lost—how well we remember that the prodigal son was lost when he strayed away from home. He was then in servitude—in the bondage of sin. When he came to himself at the "hog pen," he was in his solitude. When he arrived at his father's house and received a warm greeting, he became filled with gratitude.

There is a time for gratitude. When things go well with you and God has met your need, it is time to seek Jesus in a spirit of gratitude. Many worship and give thanks to the wrong god. Many are living a life of joy in the Spirit today. We know that we are in the last days and the coming of Christ is *imminent*. All the signs both positive and negative point to his coming.

> This know also, that in the last days perilous times shall come. For men shall be lovers of their own selves, covetous, boasters, proud, blasphemers, disobedient to parents, unthankful, unholy, without natural affection, trucebreakers, false accusers, incontinent, fierce, despisers of those that are good, traitors, heady, highminded, lovers of pleasures more than lovers of God; having a form of godliness, but denying the power thereof: from such turn away (2 Timothy 3:1-5).

Despite the evils of our times, the Spirit of God is moving in our land. During a visit to South Dakota, I heard the witness of a motel clerk who unashamedly said, "I believe in God. I have found peace with God. My husband has found him also. When he saw the change in me, he decided that if it's good enough for me, it is good enough for him."

Then, there was a smiling waitress who joyfully gave her testimony, "I'm a believer. I was born a Roman Catholic, but my girl friend witnessed to me using Romans 10:9: 'That if thou shalt confess with thy mouth the Lord Jesus, and shalt believe in thine heart that God hath raised him from the dead, thou shalt be saved.'"

There is no doubt that God is moving through his Spirit in the hearts of men in this land—all over this land and country. The darker the days become, the brighter will be his appearing. We are facing the fulfillment of prophecy:

> But this is that which was spoken by the prophet Joel; and it shall come to pass in the last days, saith God, I will pour out of my Spirit upon all flesh: and your sons and your daughters shall prophesy, and your young men shall see visions, and your old men shall dream dreams (Acts 2:16-17).

Servitude, Solitude, and Gratitude—through it all we have learned to trust in God.

Jesus tells us in his own words that he's coming again.

> But when I, the Messiah, shall come in my glory, and all the angels with me,

then I shall sit upon my throne of glory. And all the nations shall be gathered before me. And I shall separate the people as a shepherd, separate the sheep from the goats, and place the sheep at my right hand and the goats at my left.

Then I, the king, shall say to those at my right, come, blessed of my Father, into the kingdom prepared for you from the founding of the world. For I was hungry and you fed me; I was thirsty and you gave me water; I was a stranger and you invited me into your homes; naked and ye clothed me; sick and in prison, and you visited me (see Matthew 25:31-36).

"My Lord, what a morning when the stars begin to fall!" You're going to need somebody on your bond.

Christ, the Center of History

Caesar A. W. Clark

The Hebrew-Christian faith is basically historical. A review of the great Jewish and Christian historians and theologians will quickly affirm the historical nature of the faith. Turning to secular historians, one finds that history is the human effort to understand one's self in the light of what has gone before.

Unlike the flowers—which live out their cycles under God's sun with no concept of time—man measures his life in hours. He knows of birth and death—of past—present and future. Since man is an historical being and not simply an aspect of nature, he can orient himself to his historical existence in various ways. Philosophies of history come packaged in various sizes and shapes—and everyone has one.

From the simple remark, "Everything will turn out all right," to the complicated dialectical materialism of Karl Marx—a theory of history is in operation. There are historical pessimisms and

Caesar A. W. Clark is a life member of the National Baptist Convention, U.S.A., and Executive Editor of the *National Baptist Voice*. Pastor of the Good Street Baptist Church of Dallas, Texas, he is also active in a number of civic organizations.

optimisms and activisms; and somewhere in one of these "isms" everyone can be found.

In the Bible one finds a surprising variety of historical world views: the skepticism of Ecclesiastes, the pragmatism of Deuteronomy, the theological optimism of Second Isaiah, the variety in the New Testament with Paul's quasi-predestinarianism, Matthew's apocalypticism, and John's dualism. A study of Indian religious philosophy reveals that time is insignificant to the East Asian mind. To know at what point of time one's life emerges and then fades again is of no interest or importance since, presumably, one can be equally near to God at any and all points of time. Anywhere, anytime, in mystical ascent man can break through and unite his tiny being with the Absolute.

The same attitude confronts us in Fichte, the philosopher, when he says "only the metaphysical saves us—not the historical." According to this view, an historical event can illustrate a truth, but it cannot be the basis of truth. In the bibilical witness of the prophets and apostles a totally different view of time and history confronts us.

Here time is not seen as a circular sea—on whose shores anywhere man can have equally wonderful visions of God. Time is rather like a mystic meandering stream that constantly pushes forward until through the power of God it has reached its goal in the consummation of all things!

There are times when nothing significant happens. Then there are times when events may occur that impel the current of history forward. And whenever such an event has occurred, everything thereafter is different! It is then impossible to ignore the events or to turn back the clock as if this had not happened.

The freeing of the children of Israel from Egyptian bondage—the giving of the law by Moses and Aaron—the institution of Judges and Kings—the destruction of the temple at Jerusalem by Nebuchadnezzar—the Babylonian exile of the defeated people—the return of the Jews to their old homeland—these are all to be seen as stations along the road that have become of crucial significance in the relationship of the chosen people to God. The same historical consciousness confronts us in the life of Jesus Christ.

Jesus says, "My time—my hour—is not yet come." That mysterious phrase can refer both to the cross and to his glorious exaltation at the right hand of God. "And I, if I be lifted up from the earth, will draw all men unto me" (John 12:32).

Paul gives the historical event of Jesus Christ cataclysmic importance. He says, "But when the fulness of time was come, God sent forth his Son, made of a woman, made under the law, to redeem them that were under the law, that we might receive the adoption of sons" (Galatians 4:4-5).

This text takes us straight from Luke's statement of the facts of time and place, "Jesus was born at Bethlehem when Cyrenius was governor of Syria," to the deeper level of that inner world of God.

It takes us from the historical fact, "Jesus was born," to the illumination from the inner world of meaning and decision, "God sent forth his Son." And then—in case we should imagine that, after all, we are talking about some mystic event that didn't really happen in the world we know—the words are added, "born of a woman—born under the law." Under the impact and impress of the works of Jesus, the apostles and their followers proclaimed—first—that *the ultimate and invisible God was seen on this earth in the flesh and blood of a normal human life.*

Because God in the life of Christ intervened mightily in history, the letter to the Romans is able to assert and proclaim the historical juncture, "the night is far spent—the day is at hand." The old world order is shaken in its foundations—God's new age has dawned! God has taken the initiative!

The early Christian concentrated proclamation was: The Eternal God whom no man has seen or can see—who lives in a light that no man can approach—has unveiled himself and in an unmistakable manifestation of indispensable grace, the inaudible has become audible—the invisible has become visible—the intangible has become tangible—the irreproachable has become accessible! In Colossians 1:15, Christ is called "the image of the invisible God." In Hebrews 1:3, he bears the seal of majesty, "the brightness of his glory." In Matthew 11:27, Jesus' witness to himself confronts us, "neither knoweth any man the Father, save the Son, and he to whomsoever the Son will reveal him." In John 14:9, Jesus tells us "he that hath seen me hath seen the Father."

> Veiled in flesh the Godhead see;
> Hail the incarnate Deity;

> Pleased as man with men to dwell,
> Jesus, our Emmanuel.[1]

Jesus was the revelation of God—and this revelation was illumination—"For God was in Christ." This revelation was the opportunity for renewal—God makes thunder his chariot and lightning his sword pleading at man's door for reconciliation. This revelation was challenge requiring response and decision. For because of this revelation, one's attitude changes—manifesting itself in acceptance or rejection!

Jesus Christ is the center of history.

Jesus Christ is "the hinge of history."

For He takes all times off their hinges and becomes himself the Lord of time.

"Now unto the King eternal, immortal, invisible, the only wise God, be honour and glory for ever and ever. Amen" (1 Timothy 1:17).

As Lord of time he holds all moments together in the coherence of his eternal and unchanging Being! (See Colossians 1:17.) To know who he is means to have a history. For history is life with a meaning—and only one who is at the beginning and at the end of time—only one who is the Lord of time—holds all times together. Only he who is the fullness of time fills time with the ultimate meaning that constitutes it as history!

In Jesus Christ, the "I Am" of the Old Testament becomes the "Thou Art" of the New Testament.

The central self-disclosure of God in history and through history is "the word made flesh."

In contrast to Gnostic syncretism, it is said of Christ, "For it pleased the Father that in him should all fulness dwell" (Colossians 1:19). In Jesus Christ it was not simply a ray of the light of the glory of God that penetrated time. God turned himself fully toward man in this life that was "full of grace and truth." Thus it seems devious and superfluous to look elsewhere for the fullness of the knowledge of God!

Jesus is the simplification of God. All great discoveries are simplifications. The great simplification took place in Bethlehem of Judea. The "Word" became flesh. The "Word" is the expression of

[1] Charles Wesley, "Hark! The Herald Angels Sing."

the hidden thought. Jesus Christ—the "Word"—is the expression of the hidden thought—God! This word is not spelled out—it is lived out! Jesus Christ is the speech of eternity translated into the language of time!

Mystery of mysteries—God in a child calling the world up and back to him in the whimper of a baby—making him our eternal contemporary and signaling at midnight the coming of a new power and a new glory into the hearts and lives of men which could make them redeemed sons of the living God. Mystery of mysteries—the Divine approach was not by any drama of terrorism—but by a drama of tenderness—by the appeal of a little child. With what homely gentleness the eternal God stole into our midst! Of all the births the world ever knew, none has so stirred the imagination, so appealed to the poetic impulse, and so thrilled the heart of humanity as the birth of Jesus. It has caused more pictures to be painted, more poems to be written, more literature to be produced, more discussions by philosophical and polemic minds than any other birth in history. Jesus did not become a King—he was born a King. His birth was proclaimed by prophets, announced by angels, sung by shepherds, and wondered at by wise men.

When the proper time had fully come—God sent forth his Son— born of a woman—born subject to the regulations of the Law, to purchase the freedom of—to redeem—to atone for—those who were subject to the Law—that we might be adopted and have sonship conferred upon us—be recognized as God's sons.

To the message of God's incarnation in the Logos become flesh, the apostles and their followers proclaimed in the second place: *The word of reconciliation—the Saviorhood of Christ.* He stands in the center of history as the only Savior from sin!

He came to "seek and save the lost." His coming was an invasion of history from beyond history in order to redeem history!

The Swedish theologian Gustaf Wingren took vigorous issue with Karl Barth that the human predicament is not only that we have removed ourselves from God and no longer know who or what God is. The greatest need of our existence is due to the fact that we are imprisoned under the despotic rule of a power that is against God— and that will not release us and from which we by our own efforts cannot extricate ourselves! We have not fully understood the implications of the coming of Jesus into history if we glorify him only as the revealer of the Father!

Jesus Christ must be recognized as the one who appeared in history to destroy the works of the devil! Christ stands in the center of history as God's cardinal redemptive act! In the light of Christ the Old Testament becomes the "dawn of world redemption." It began when Abraham was taken out of a heathen environment—out of a world of polytheism and astrology—that he might heed the God who justifies the guilty and raises the dead. Like Abraham in his time the nation born of His seed is—through judgment and grace—brought by God into a holy discipline. But when Christ came to his own, they received him not. They cast him out and made a cross for him!

They ridiculed and rejected him!

They humiliated and harassed him!

They castigated and crucified him!

Christ's death on the cross is a fact of history! The immediate contemporaries who witnessed Christ's death on the cross did not automatically interpret it as a victory for law and order. How could a bystander in Jerusalem watching one of the innumerable executions beyond the city wall detect the crucifixion of Christ as an event of decisiveness for all history? Even by Christ's own disciples it was mourned as a defeat!

The New Testament gospel is not simply that Christ died—rather, the gospel of the New Testament is the Good News that Christ died for our sins and rose again for our justification!

Rudolph Bultmann is wrong when he denies that these facts of historical revelation can be certified only through subjective experience!

The saving "event" must be proclaimed through the saving "communication" before the divine-human encounter can take place.

The "mighty acts" of God in Christ constitute "Event Revelation." The truth of Christ as revealed by the Holy Spirit constitutes "Word Revelation." Gospel truth does not stem from merely human impulses. The divine revelation of the Holy Spirit is the source of gospel truth! The gospel preacher has been commissioned by Christ as his mouthpiece to proclaim the Word Revelation, and this Word Revelation stands alongside the "mighty acts" of God in Christ as part of the historical process of divine redemption!

The gospel preacher is somewhat like a tape recorder—and he must see to it that he adequately and accurately receives and records and communicates the "truth-revelation."

The apostles and their followers proclaimed in the third place: *The reality of the resurrection. The resurrection is the presence of the exalted Christ.*

By his resurrection Christ inaugurated eschatological history and became its "first fruits." The resurrection of Christ is more than a past historical event—it is a history-making present reality! The resurrection of Christ in preaching is joined to the crucifixion not by calendar time, because when he appears in history, history comes to an end in its old form, and the last—the eschatological—age begins. When Reinhold Niebuhr says the eschaton is "beyond history," he does not mean it is unhistorical, but rather that it is not a product of world history—but the "end" of world history.

When Rudolph Bultmann says "all history is swallowed up in eschatology," he does not mean that eschatology has nothing to do with history—but rather that it is the event which gives all history its new point of beginning!

Jesus Christ—the risen, reigning Savior—stands at the midpoint of history as the end of one world and the beginning of a new history! Because of the resurrection of Christ a new power has been let loose in the world.

This power has changed more lives for God and good. This power has transformed more barren deserts into flower gardens—more sighs into songs—more gloom into glory—more fear into faith—more dark nights of despair into days bright with hope—more weakness into strength—more burdens into blessings—more deadness into life—more sadness into gladness—more tragedies into triumphs—more mourns into joys—more confusion into calm—more corruption into purity and extracted the sting of death from more dying pillows than any other power known to mankind!

Theologically speaking, B.C. is not an epoch of time that ended with the birth of Christ—it is a condition of living. Whoever is not subject to the lordship of Christ is living in B.C. Whoever is not conscious of the presence of Christ in daily living is living in B.C.

Eschatological history terminates the protracted hopelessness of existential history. Eschatological history is the revelation to world history that history has a future—a hope—an ultimate meaning!

Jesus Christ fills the paratactic gaps in existential history and himself becomes the hinge of history—dispersing despair with hope!

The presence of God in Christ is the difference between existential and eschatological history!

The resurrection of Jesus Christ is the pivotal doctrine of the Christian faith—for the witness of the New Testament declares that "if Christ has not been raised—your faith is futile and you are still in your sins."

Whether it be regarded as veritable history—convenient mythology—or a deliberate hoax—the resurrection is inescapable. One can neither assert nor deny the truth of the Christian gospel without taking cognizance of this fundamental article of belief!

Opposition has focused on three points: The integrity of literary sources, the intrinsic historic probability of the narrative, and the scientific possibility of such a phenomenon. The evidence is sufficient to demonstrate from a literary-historical—and scientific—viewpoint that something happened that can be classed as an objective "Event" and that left an ineradicable imprint on the lives and faith of the early believers. Their attitudes, characters, and careers were transformed, and the church which resulted from their new faith still persists as a movement in history!

The "event-character" of the resurrection is unaffected by faith or unbelief! The resurrection is an affirmation of the biblical realism of objective revelation in history!

The Risen Christ stands in the center of history to reveal to man what it means to be a man!

Christ stands in the center of history elucidating the dialectical tension in the life of God!

Christ stands in the center of history as a "happening" in the midst of a people—a happening in time. He both connects and separates the Old and the New—the past and the future!

Christ stands in the center of history as our Reconciler!

Christ stands in the center of history as our Restorer!

Christ stands in the center of history as our Redeemer!

Christ stands in the center of history as the Creator of our history and the source of our meaningful life!

Christ stands in the center of history to fill the paratactic gaps without which our life is all in pieces and all coherence is gone!

Christ stands in the center of history, quickening man's historical consciousness and destroying the pockets of meaninglessness in existential history!

Christ stands in the center of history as the Presence—the very act of God! God is present in history in Christ!

And where God is present, existential history is given an end and life is caught up in eschatological history!

Existential history is a phenomenon in world history. Eschatological history is a phenomenon in biblical history where events which have finality give history the form of its existence. In Christ the beginning and the end—the "archeo" and "telos"—of history occur. World history comes to an end in the sense of being transcended by a higher history. Even biblical history comes to an end—henceforth Jesus Christ is the source and possibility of a history where hopelessness is once and for all overcome. Jesus Christ is the form and the content of the event through which God now calls the world to decide and by that call precipitates the new age of eschatological history!

Christ stands in the center of history as the cornerstone that God has laid with the immovable significance of eternity in the swaying foundations of this world!

Jesus Christ is the redemption of history. He gives it focus—brings it under judgment—and grants it grace. He left a throne, entered history, and found a cross! "The word became flesh"—a piece of history—"and tented among us." Though we be wicked and wretched—doomed and defiled—poor and despised—through the Son of God we have a chance to become sons of God! We have a chance to have sonship conferred upon us! We have a chance to be recognized as God's sons!

A FINAL WORD

The revelation of God!

The response of man!

The greatest sin of man is not his rebellion against God—but his refusal to respond to God's appeal!

To respond is to exercise "saving faith in Jesus Christ as the only begotten Son of God!"

To respond is to repent—to change the mind—to turn from to!
To respond is to enlist in the army of the living God!
To respond is to commit oneself to Christ in faith—in love—in service.
To respond is to seek and obey the truth of God in Christ!
To respond is to experience newness and renewal through Christ!
To respond is to experience a new state of being—"in Christ"!

IN CHRIST WE HAVE

A Life that can never be forfeited.
A Relation that can never be abrogated.
A Righteousness that can never be tarnished.
An Acceptance that can never be questioned.
A Judgment that can never be repeated.
A Title that can never be clouded.
A Position that can never be invalidated.
A Standing that can never be disputed.
A Justification that can never be reversed.
A Seal that can never be violated.
An Inheritance that can never be alienated.
A Wealth that can never be depleted.
A Resource that can never be diminished.
A Bank that can never be closed.
A Possession that can never be measured.
A Portion that can never be denied.
A Peace that can never be destroyed.
A Joy that can never be suppressed.
A Love that can never be abated.
A Grace that can never be arrested.
A Strength that can never be vitiated.
A Power that can never be exhausted.
A Salvation that can never be annulled.
A Forgiveness that can never be rescinded.
A Deliverance that can never be disavowed.
As Assurance that can never be disappointed.
A Nature that can never be changed.
A Comfort that can never be lessened.
An Attraction that can never be superseded.

An Access that can never be discontinued.
A Service that can never be unrewarded.
An Intercessor who can never be disqualified.
A Revelation that can never be impeached.
A Victor who can never be vanquished.
A Glory that can never be dimmed.
A Hope that can never be disappointed.
A Resurrection that can never be hindered!

Following Pilate's Path of Futility

Strobridge E. Hoard

Isaiah 53

Once again, God has spared us to come to the edge of Easter. By his grace and mercy, we find ourselves living during another Easter season.

I never approach this sacred moment without being reminded of Jesus and his disciples—Peter, James, and John—when he led them to a high mountain. There, before them, he was transfigured. He was changed. Peter recognized that something great, something important had happened; thus he said to the Master: "Lord, it is well that we are here; if you wish [Master], I will make three booths [tabernacles] here, one for you and one for Moses and one for Elijah" (Matthew 17:4, RSV).

If I might use the words of this disciple, I say to you: It is well that

Strobridge E. Hoard graduated from Kentucky State College, Hampton Institute, Virginia Union Seminary, and received a D.D. from Simmons University, Louisville, Kentucky. He was pastor of State Street Baptist Church, Bowling Green, Kentucky, and the Tabernacle Baptist Church, Dayton, Ohio.

we are here—not to build three tabernacles, but to look intro-spectively into our lives. We are here to search our Christian character, to see how we can improve it. It is well that we are here to work on a building not made by mortal hands.

May God grant us the vision to see ourselves through the character, the faults, and failures of Pontius Pilate. May the Almighty save us from Pilate's path of futility and lead us fully into his service.

I

As we listen to the voice of the unforgotten past, the Prophet Isaiah gives thoughts for this moment, for the future:

> Surely he has borne our griefs
>   and carried our sorrows . . .
> But he was wounded for our transgressions,
>   he was bruised for our iniquities
> upon him was the chastisement that made us whole,
>   and with his stripes we are healed.
>
> Isaiah 53:4-5, RSV.

Isaiah reminds us: "All we like sheep have gone astray; we have turned every one to his own way."

These words have ripened with time and conflict. They indict us. They call attention to the gift of Jesus Christ, to his sacrifice on our behalf. So, in moments like these, at a time like this when we search our souls—these words challenge the best and worst in us. They issue a mandate to look toward Calvary, to look at the plight of our neighbor, to look at ourselves in order that we may move forward with Christ.

In other words, life must have a real meaning. We can find that meaning only through Christ Jesus. All other roads lead to futility.

No wonder our world is torn asunder by conflicts of every kind. No wonder our church is threatened by godless communism. Is it any wonder that many of our churches stand at the brink of closing? That many people no longer find God a necessity, but a luxury?

Right today, many Christians of every kind and order are finding life confusing. Many feel that they can't go on. Their crosses are too heavy; their burdens are wearing them down. God has gone from them.

But the truth of the matter is, we have strayed like sheep. One of the greatest fears and problems of our time is that we might not be of any real value to the world. We fear being of no real value to ourselves. We dread coming upon the stage of life, playing no real part, and then fading away like a vapor.

Brethren, make no mistake about it. Futility is a terrible force. It's a threat to our Christian life. It often causes us to stand before ourselves in fear. It often causes us to stand before our neighbor and God in fear and trembling, sick unto death no matter how strong we are. Sometimes, we act like we don't know where to turn for power and grace.

I like to read Ecclesiastes. The writer points up, he drives home, the tragedy of vain living, of walking the path of futility.

Life and all of its struggles, all of its sorrows, and all of its ups and downs becomes miserable, and the grave its goal.

Jesus came that we might have the good life, and have it more abundantly. He came that we might have spiritual eyes to see our way clearly. He came that we would not have to drift like broken clouds, but so we can keep him as the apple of our eye, the way of life, our truth.

Jesus has set before us certain responsibilities and tasks that we cannot escape. He did not command us to be like Pilate, but to be unlike him. Therefore, each man is called, at least, to the task of being responsible, of standing firm in those things which are righteous, honest, and just. As Jesus said: "Not my will, but thine be done." To follow any other path is to lose your purpose in life.

II

I have often dreamed of being a great painter—one of the subjects I would like to put on canvas would be that of a lost soul. There is no sight more horrible, no soul more confused, than that person whose life is drifting down streams of nothingness.

Pilate was such a person who followed this path, who failed to stand firm in right things. Pilate was the fifth governor of Judea. And to history, certainly to Christianity, he would have meant nothing—except that our Lord and Master stood before him to be judged; our Lord worked, suffered, and died under this man.

Like a mighty blacksmith, striking his heavy hammer against a hard anvil, Pilate struck the blow; he issued the order, though silently, that condemned Jesus. He was the trigger to this tragic, yet glorious, occasion.

We recognize the fact that he should not bear all the blame. For surely there were others in this drama of human suffering. Caiaphas, the high priest, must stand as the plotter, Judas as the deceiver, and the soldiers as executioners—all must be found guilty, too. Regardless, each man, each person, must be responsible for his own personal conduct, his own divine destiny.

Men throughout history have asked: Why did Pilate surrender Jesus after finding him not guilty? Why didn't he stand up for what he believed? Did he really believe he could wash the guilty stain from his life by merely saying, "I am innocent of this righteous man's blood"?

Man has no right to judge his brother. Yet man's failures and successes are judged by the tracks left upon the sands of time. History reveals Pilate was a man who thought he could carry a bucket of water on each shoulder, without spilling a drop.

For instance, when Pilate was first appointed governor of Judea, he allowed his soldiers to establish idolatry in Jerusalem. Caesar was the god of Pilate and the soldiers; but when the Jews objected to the practice of idolatry within their holy city, then Pilate removed the image of his god from Jerusalem. In other words, any man who kicks his own god out because of fear of criticism, because of opposition, is a man of weak conviction. He is a Pilate.

In the second place—Pilate wore a robe of instability. He trod the path of indecision. He was not a Nicodemus who wanted to be changed. He was not a Nicodemus who encountered Jesus in his personal life, by the water and the spirit. Pilate was not a Paul, who met his Master on the Damascus Road. He was not a Martin Luther, or a Martin Luther King, for that matter. He would not say, "Here I stand; God have mercy on me."

Pilate was like many of us—like many of us on the church rolls. He thought he could please everyone and God, too. How often we Christians drift upon this cloud of impossibility and are carried by these winds of instability!

When Jesus was accused by the priests and officers of the Sanhedrin, Pilate refused to be moved by the charge that Jesus was a disturber of the peace. Here, he had his chance to be a Nicodemus, to be transformed. But acting true to pattern, when a more powerful charge was made against Jesus, he gave up. When Pilate was put on trial too, when his life was in jeopardy, when his exalted position was challenged, he was torn asunder by indecision. He couldn't make up his mind.

The only way he saw out of his maze was to escape making a decision by sending Jesus to Herod. Again, he failed to find an escape over the path of futility.

Pilate got a second chance—Herod forced him to do something with Jesus. For a while Pilate held firm. But when the unrelenting bigots would not retreat, he allowed Barrabas to go free and Jesus to be crucified.

He had turned over individual responsibility to other people. He acted as though it was not his decision to make. Did he have the authority? Did he not sell his birthright? Surely Pilate suffered a severe breakdown in human personality; he sinned.

His sin let him think that he was innocent. Instead he should have cried out, like this Negro spiritual:

It's not my sister or my brother,
but it's me, O Lord, standing in
the need of prayer.

Or, it's not the crowd, but it's me, Pilate, standing in the need of prayer.

III

History and the church have seen Pilate become the judge.

By judging Jesus, he became judged himself. He was the real defendant on trial. Not Jesus, but Pilate! He who would have gained much by this transaction stands out as the despised, the smitten, the lonely and rejected. And no longer Jesus, but the Romans, the Jews, the Sanhedrin Court, and Pilate are on trial.

We Christians, right today, face the same act of history as we seek to release Barrabas and to crucify Jesus daily. As we face a confused, frightened mankind, needful of God's love and understanding, we forsake the real self, the spiritual being in us, and leave our destiny up to the desperate, crying crowds, crying out, "Crucify him! Crucify Jesus!"

No longer, then, is the Master of life on trial at Jerusalem, but we all are on trial; the bigots, the human courts, the shallow compromises, the laws, and, yes, even the church stands at the bar of divine justice, with Jesus as the real judge.

Therefore, we are confronted with two powerful questions as we seek to walk in the right path.

There is the question the governor asked the crowd, the question that still echoes through the corridors of time, even unto generations yet unborn: "People, what then will ye do with Jesus?"

The other query resounds under the listening sky to each of us, "What then will ye let Jesus do with your life?"

Make no mistake about it—Pilate could have been forgiven, made whole. For there is a hope for all those who, like sheep, go astray.

As Jesus would say: "Father, forgive them, for they know not what they do."

Father, forgive Judas, my betrayer!

Father, forgive Pilate, too. Teach them the power of love, the real value of life.

Pilate's anxiety to avoid offense to Caesar, his god—to save himself from harm—certainly did not save him from political disaster. The power he loved was gone, the prize he sought lost.

As Jesus would say: "What does it profit a man, if he shall gain the whole world, and lose his soul?" Too often, we are like Pilate!

Governor Pilate did not gain the world, and yet he lost his soul. What happened to this confused, this sinful man?

Well, tradition takes up the drama where the Bible leaves off. It claims that Pilate sought to hide his sorrows on a mountain, somewhere near Lake Lucerne. And even though he spent many years on that mountain, in deep remorse and despair, he never really repented. Just as though he had not wasted a good life by following the path of vainglory, he added to it another sin by plunging himself into the dismal lake near the mountain to complete his death, to end the path that leads nowhere.

I am sure that anyone with a forgiving heart, with a Christlike spirit, would have found himself, somewhere along the road, would have found himself before it was too late. I am sure many Christians would hope that Pilate could have been another Nicodemus, who was there to help Jesus down from the cross, to help bury his body in the tomb; or if he could have been like Paul, or even like Judas, the betrayer, who repented before filling his grave. But, no, Pilate took the wrong path home, the road of futility.

In conclusion, my Christian brethren, this story is told over and over, not because it is new. For really it is old as the flow of blood in human veins.

It's told because it concerns us, concerns our lives. Right today the church of Jesus Christ stands before the Governor. Right today, each of us is on trial.

We still hear the ancient questions pounding in our ears: "Whom shall we release? Or, "What will we let him do with us?" Or, "What will we let him do with me?"

The reply is not Pilate's any longer, but it is ours. As we decide, not once—but every second, every day of our lives, in every experience— let us not be afraid to serve the Lord.

Let us not be afraid of making real sacrifices in his name. Let us recommit ourselves to his keeping. Don't be afraid or ashamed to do great things for God, with God, and certainly for God's people.

As Isaiah, the prophet, wrote centuries ago when he was encouraging his people, today we hear him saying, "Surely he has borne our griefs, and carried our sorrows."

If God has done this once, and I know he has, certainly God will still continue to grant his grace and mercy to those who serve well. Surely he would not leave us alone even in conflict, even in sorrow, or even in death. God loves those who serve him.

So let us follow him all the way, from earth to heaven, even though it will be a cross.

Jesus assures us:

> If anyone wishes to be a follower of mine, he must leave self behind. He must take up his cross and come with me. Whoever cares for his safety is lost; but if a man will let himself be lost for my sake, he will find his true self. (See Matthew 16:24-25.)

And finally, brethren, quoting from Albert Schweitzer's *The Quest of the Historical Jesus:*

> He [meaning Jesus] comes to us as One unknown, without a name, as of old, by the lake-side, He came to those men who knew Him not. He speaks to us the same word: "Follow thou me!" and sets us to the tasks which He

has to fulfil for our time. He commands. And to those who obey Him, whether they be wise or simple, He will reveal Himself in the toils, the conflicts, the sufferings which they shall pass through in His fellowship. . . .[1]

[1] Albert Schweitzer, *The Quest of the Historical Jesus* (New York: Macmillan, Inc., 1961), p. 403.

Come Before Winter

Walter B. Hoard

2 Timothy 4:21

Let us think together about a scriptural experience that says something informative and truthful to us.

Let me draw from the experiences of one of God's men—an apostle—as he revealed himself as a worthy servant in 2 Timothy 4:21. Let me use as a subject, "Come Before Winter." In this epistle note that Paul leaves one of the most impressive charges, challenges, ever given to a servant of the Lord.

Do you recall that Paul had been like a father to Timothy, this young man? *Do you recall,* Paul was responsible for leading Timothy to Christ and taught him his first lesson about the Master from Galilee? He carried Timothy with him on certain missionary journeys in order that he might see and learn how the church functions; how much the church is *spread abroad;* how work is carried on by a few

Walter B. Hoard is Executive Dean of the Chicago Baptist Institute. Former positions have included the post of Associate General Secretary of the American Baptist Churches in the U.S.A. and the pastorate of churches in Rhode Island, Wisconsin, and New York.

committed dedicated, faithful Christian servants in each place.

Paul had a purpose in guiding Timothy. In the first place, the church needed more men like Timothy. Paul was ending his earthly journey, his Christian mission, and he knew God would soon call him home. But the faith, the church, the kingdom of God, if these were meaningful to human life—then, the church had to be developed among *all* men. If it meant anything, then the faith had to be spread abroad. If the church was going to lead men to God, then it had to recruit men like Timothy and train them.

Of course, Paul had no desire to quit. He was going to serve God till he died. Surely he didn't even want to die. Regardless of his desire to stay here longer, to preach good news to the poor, to set at liberty the oppressed—regardless, Paul knew his time was almost at hand.

We might say it was the autumn, the fall of Paul's life. The *spring* had come and gone—like the melody of a beautiful song. Now that it was the autumn of this servant's life, the leaves which turned golden in the sunset were falling. The summer had come and the harvest passed, and all that was left were the thoughts of spring's refreshing views, summer's dreams, a few victories, and many failures.

So soon the winter season, the final season, would sit on the doorsteps of Paul's life. *The end was in sight.* Winter, with all its fury, peculiarities, with all *its threats,* with all its finality, was approaching quickly. So Paul in prison wrote to Timothy, telling him, "Don't tarry! Don't wait. Do your best to come to me soon. Do your best to come before winter." "Summer has passed; the harvest is ended; we are not yet ready." God knows.

Paul had faced winter before—it wasn't new. It wasn't as if he lived on the sunny shores of Florida and suddenly moved to the frigid shores of Maine, or from the hot Delta of Mississippi to cold, windy Chicago. But in serving God *Paul had been on the ocean,* in distant lands, in winter's cold and summer's heat, spreading the gospel, starting churches; so the chilly winds of winter were not new to him.

But, you say, if Paul had faced winter before, why was it, or what was it that made this season so important? What was the urgency? Why did he insist that Timothy come soon? Before winter? Quickly? Well, no one has to tell us here in *Chicago about the winter season*— we know it is cold—lots of snow. We need plenty of heat. Our bills get higher. Old cars get cantankerous, like some people—don't want to start. Sometimes they make you lose your religion. *Roads get slippery*—you have to drive with care. Surely winter is a peculiar season—there are so many adjustments we have to make for winter—even though it comes every year. Let me illustrate. I remember my first year pastoring in New York State, *where some places the temperature gets to 60 below zero.* The first year there, I put anti-freeze in my car—like I was supposed to. I got it ready to endure bad weather, as usual. But one Sunday morning I came out the door, and the snow was two feet high. I shoveled that. I jumped in my car—a brand new car—but it wouldn't start. I tried everything! I couldn't imagine what was wrong. That wasn't my first winter—but something was wrong with the car. It wouldn't run! Soon I realized I had *not* winterized my car for upstate New York. It was all right in Rhode Island—but I hadn't gotten ready for this particular winter. To paraphrase Shakespeare: This was my *winter of discontent.* Make no mistake about it, our winter of discontent is approaching rapidly. Soon we will feel its discomforts. As Paul said, "Timothy, try to come to me soon! Let's do something for God, before this terrible season comes upon us. Don't wait." Come over to Rome soon!

One reason why I like this episode in Paul's life is because it says something meaningful to us today. First, he stresses a sense of urgency. Do it now! Don't wait! Notice, Paul was in Rome alone, except for Luke. He needed help. Demas had left him, had forsaken him. No matter how committed Paul was to Jesus, he couldn't do it *all* alone. As John Donne said: *"No man is an island."* Paul wanted some help; he wanted it soon. As Jesus said, "The harvest is great, but the laborers are few."

The church is no different today; it needs help. Sometimes I look around our churches and ask, "Where did all the men go?" When I pastored, I tried to rationalize it. *I said women* must be more loyal to God than men. At times I've thought maybe women *need* more religion than men. But now, I'm beginning to believe, much of our trouble in the world is because men have gained the world and lost their souls. We don't take God seriously. One thing is certain, when we get to heaven, there won't be a big crowd up there. I feel the same way about our men sometimes. For instance, some asked Jesus if they would see their wife or husband when they get to heaven. *Jesus said, "There won't be any marrying in heaven."* I understand why now—

because there won't be but a few men up there. *You know, for some reason* I believe God knew what he was doing—when he made man! *"Putting every living thing in subjection under his feet."* I don't want *to start a revolution,* but let's tell it like it is. Nevertheless, men had better learn to protect their manhood. A classmate of mine, when a boy, listened to his grandmother reading the Bible, the second chapter of Hebrews, where it says, "What is man. . . ." He asked her, "Grandma, what is man?" Chewing tobacco, she didn't look up from her Bible. She simply paused and said, "Son, man is breath and britches, more breath than britches."

Sometimes we do act like breath. Not like men! I have to laugh at black women, who talk about women's lib. Black women have always been freer! *But I don't laugh at our men*—who can't stand on two feet. To be certain, there ARE MEN WHO WORK EIGHT HOURS A DAY, BUT HAVE TO ASK THEIR WIFE FOR 50 CENTS. "Baby, is it alright if I buy a coke?" For me, if I am big enough to work every day, then I don't carry my check home to any woman and ask her for 50 cents of my money to buy a coke. You see, the tragic influence about this kind of thinking and acting is that it doesn't stop in your house. It spreads all over into our church, community, race. It affects our youth—our whole life! To be sure, there are too many church officers who spend other folks' money, but can't spend their own. They don't handle money at home, but feel qualified to control church money. Poor management. Don't you know, if you can't administer your own money, you can't handle mine. There are many people who feel like me, but keep silent or refuse to give to the church because of this reason.

Now is the time to revolutionize our communities by changing our church. For you see, this attitude spreads abroad to our *black business* everywhere!

For certain, you have seen some of our business places. Not all, but some. If you go into a restaurant to buy a hamburger—the waitress throws it on the table at you. But she wants a tip, even though she was angry because she had to take your order. In other restaurants you have to wait all day to spend your money! This is deplorable. This is a terrible winter! *As Paul said, "Timothy, come soon, come before winter."* Time is urgent! Don't tarry! Paul wanted this young man to come over to Rome soon, before it was too late. He needed the chance to talk with Paul. "So, Timothy, servant of the Lord, if you want to learn how to best serve Christ and his church, don't wait! Come now!"

You know, there are many people who live like they had a thousand years to live—no sense of urgency! Yet, they are in the *autumn of life* and can't see winter will soon come. Perhaps they don't believe it! Paul knew the *value of* time. He had wasted many precious years fighting against the church. He wished somehow he could turn back the hand of time. But now all he could do was to use the time he had left, and *impress* upon others to use theirs. *Don't wait,* for winter will come soon. I'm always amazed at people who argue that you can be *saved*—on your dying bed, with your last breath. I suppose they are right—because God will answer any sinner's cry for salvation, anytime or anywhere. *But I think a person is wrong;* I think it's a sin to wait until the edge of fall—when winter is just upon them—to cry out for God's mercy, especially when people use the best years of their lives doing what they want, then come to God with the crumbs, broken and worn, no energy or much time left to serve him.

I wouldn't advise any man to procrastinate, to waste his life—saying, "Tomorrow, I'll come to God. Tomorrow, I'll call on Jesus. I have plenty of time! The harvest is past, the summer is ended, and I'm not yet ready, but I'll wait, anyhow!"

Don't you know—it doesn't take long for winter to come—*one day,* we walk in the breezes of spring; one day, we *watch the lilies* of the valley grow. One day, we hear the chirping of *the bird,* watch *her fly on wings.* One day, we feel new, brand new. *We feel fresh as a daisy in bloom.* We are *fresh like* the morning dew. One day, *we are young* and vibrant—the world is our *playground*—full of life, hopes, dreams, visions, and expectations. As Joel said, "Old men dream dreams; young men have visions."

But for some foolish reason we think the spring of life will remain forever and ever. We think, *like the flower,* we will always blossom. Our leaf will not wither. But soon, the summer comes and passes, the fall is upon us and almost gone and only then we begin to *hurry,* to *rush,* to make *haste,* to get ready for the hardships of winter.

I am reminded of one of my favorite stories: *Tobacco Road.* If you saw the picture or read the book, you know about this poor country family. Each year the father kept saying, "Next year, *I'm going to plant my crop.* I'm going to have *tall corn, fresh fruit.* I'll sell my crop—repair my house. Get the things my family needs." But every year *when each spring came—this man sat on his porch again, rocking, waiting.* Soon the spring was gone, summer had passed—he had no harvest. But once again, he said the same thing, "Next spring, I'll plant my crop. I'll grow tall corn and so on." *So it happened—he procrastinated, waited, delayed his life* away. One day, they led him and his wife to the poorhouse. As he walked up that lonesome road of no return, he kept looking back, saying, "Someday, someday, I'm going to plant my crop." Oh, there are so many people like this in the world. There are so many people who started out once serving in the church. As the hymnologist wrote:

> Many they are who start in the race;
> But with the light they refuse to keep pace;
> Others accept it because it is new,
> But not very many expect to go through.[1]

No wonder our youth are on dope—standing around, leaning against buildings like they have to keep them from falling—doing nothing but wasting time and life. *No wonder* crime possesses the land. No wonder races still hate each other and justice is as far off as the seventh heaven. We have gained the world but lost our life. Instead of giving up, they should stand up for Jesus. I know it is hard sometimes—but we still have men who stand with Timothy, Mark, Luke, John—who with Paul, will say, "I've started in Jesus and I'm going through."

For me, I'm not going just to have my name on the church roll. I want to serve Jesus while I can. *"I may not preach* like Peter, I may not pray like Paul, but if I can help someone, traveling along the way, then my living will not be in vain."

As I said, being a man is not easy; being a Christian man is even harder. As Paul told Timothy—he also told you and me, "Come before winter!" Live while you may! Regard life as Longfellow urges. Don't wait—

> Art is long, and Time is fleeting,
> And our hearts, though stout and brave,

[1] Herbert Buffum, "I'm Going Through, Jesus," in A. M. Townsend, ed., *The Baptist Standard Hymnal* (Nashville: Sunday School Publishing Board, 1924), p. 484.

> Still, like muffled drums, are beating
> Funeral marches to the grave.[2]

But as Paul said, I know my time is not long. I'm about to be sacrificed. I know my enemies will soon put me to death; I know winter will come and go. *But I want everybody* to know: I did my best! I kept my pledge! I served my God! I've *finished* the race. *I've kept the faith.* Now, the time comes to go home to receive my crown of righteousness! I don't regret it; I thank God.

Men, I don't know about you! But for me, I'll serve God until I die. I am thankful for the time he's given me. A long time ago, I started to walk in the light—now, I'm going on through. Inflation won't stop me! Crime won't stop me! I'll let *nothing* separate me. Sometimes, I've fought a good fight. Sometimes, I failed, but I'm going through.

Oftentimes, I've run the race, and I've won. But many times, I failed to run. But I'm going through. Sometimes, I have kept the faith. But other times, I've doubted. But I'm going through. Because my Master may come *before winter.* I don't want him to pass me by. I need Jesus. I need the love of God.

[2]From "A Psalm of Life," in Henry Wadsworth Longfellow, *The Complete Poetical Works of Longfellow* (Boston: Houghton Mifflin Company, 1893), p. 3.

Faith Makes
the Difference

William A. Johnson

But Peter said, "I have no silver and gold, but I give you what I have; in the name of Jesus Christ of Nazareth, walk!" (Acts 3:6, RSV).

The account of the healing of the lame man is a journey in religious experience, a journey from begging to praising. The question is "What made the difference?" The book of the Acts of the Apostles is history; we have in it accounts of the actual happenings in the lives of the apostles as they were led and directed by the Holy Spirit, who came to them at Pentecost. So we can say of this miraculous healing of the lame man: "It happened."

Some people are inclined to think of the Bible as a collection of pieces of poetry and imaginative stories of possible events. But of this incident we can say, "It happened." And it all began in a casual sort of way as the apostle Luke reports it.

Two of the disciples, Peter and John, were going up to the temple,

William A. Johnson is pastor of the Saint John Church-Baptist in Chicago and Dean Emeritus of the Chicago Baptist Institute. He has served as president of the Church Federation of Greater Chicago as well as on other boards and interdenominational organizations.

for the three o'clock hour of prayer. There was nothing particularly significant about two apostles of Christ going to prayer meeting. They went as a matter of habit or custom. They did not announce that they would preach that day, or that they would perform any miracles. They were simply going to the temple to share in the regular prayer meeting, as we go to share in the prayer service or worship service of our church.

Of course there were some significant aspects to that ordinary situation: For example, brief mention should be made of the fact that two such different personalities as Peter and John were going together for the service of prayer at the temple.

Peter was a practical, dynamic doer of deeds; John was the idealist, the poet, the dreamer of dreams. Now they walked together in spiritual fellowship.

The coming of the Holy Spirit upon all the apostles must have made the difference in their relationship. At this point we could emphasize the necessity for the powers of the Holy Spirit to aid us in developing real Christian fellowship. For it is only by the power of the Holy Spirit that we arrive at the point when we can "share each other's woes, each other's burdens bear, and often for each other shed the sympathizing tear."

So by the Holy Spirit, two different personalities walk in Christian fellowship.

Another point we might emphasize is that Peter and John were prayer partners. I have said on other occasions, every Christian ought to have a prayer partner—a kind of praying-together pal, someone whom you can call and ask to pray with you, in a special situation.

People of the world outside of Christ have partners; they have certain people with whom they play bridge, or poker, or what have you; they have certain persons with whom they enjoy a cocktail, or what have you. . . . People of the Way—Christians—ought to have prayer partners. "If two of you agree on earth about anything they ask, it will be done for them by my Father in heaven. For where two or three are gathered in my name, there am I in the midst of them" (Matthew 18:19-20, RSV).

I think that, unless your car is filled with your own family, each of you ought to find someone in your neighborhood who does not own a car and invite that person to ride with you to church. (Of course that person should be ready when you call for him or her.)

Such an act might be the means of developing a real sincere Christian fellowship, and only God can tell what might happen if two of you agreed on what you asked of God. Our story for today is evidence of that.

Peter and John, prayer partners, were going to the temple at the usual time for afternoon prayer. . . .

At the Gate Beautiful, they met a group of men carrying a cripple. Every day they brought him there; he was a beggar as well as a cripple. Begging was a necessary activity for him; he could not work. There were no institutions like the Salvation Army or those which provide work for the handicapped, as we have in these days. There were no public relief funds available; there was only begging.

But this was a wise beggar; he picked the most profitable spot in Jerusalem to ply his trade—begging for money—the most attractive of all the gates of the temple area—the Gate Beautiful.

It was certainly a good spot for begging—or should have been. For if any people should be concerned about the needs of people, it ought to be those going to church. If any one will listen to a cry of need, one would suppose that he can find that one among the people of God— going to church to pray. For no one can pray with sincerity without thinking of others. The needs of others must be a concern of Christians.

Jesus said, "As my Father has sent me, even so I send you" (John 20:21, RSV). For what purpose did the Father send Jesus?

Jesus tells us that also: ". . . The Spirit of the Lord is upon me, because he hath anointed me to preach the gospel to the poor; he hath sent me to heal the brokenhearted, to preach deliverance to the captives, and recovering of sight to the blind, to set at liberty them that are bruised" (Luke 4:18).

Christians cannot walk easily into the temple to pray and ignore the cry of need at the gate.

The apostles Peter and John heard this beggar asking for money. Someone has suggested that we can find beggars inside the church— people who come to get something and to give nothing—people, who claim to be Christians, but have not progressed in spiritual experience past the begging stage of development.

All their prayers are begging prayers. All their words of

thanksgiving are for things received. They are always ready to receive but have nothing to give. They are beggars inside the church.

The beggar whom Peter and John met at the Gate Beautiful was simply that—a beggar, smart enough to have selected a good spot for begging, smart enough to know that people going in to pray are most likely to be in a generous mood. But that was all he was, when he called to Peter and John asking for money—a beggar!

He thought that money was the answer to his problem; he thought money was the answer to his difficulties; he thought that a gift of money was the best gift anyone could give him.

But money is not always the best gift. It is, of course, an easy way out. Peter and John could have used that easy way. Silver and gold they did not have, but perhaps one of them had a copper or two in his purse. He could have dropped that into the beggar's hand and continued his walk into the temple. That would have stilled the beggar's voice and eased their own consciences.

But what kind of a Christian is it who can drop a coin and walk away satisfied that he has done his duty?

Give money, if possible; but at the same time give something else that might tend to raise a person's self-esteem, lift his sights, arouse his interest in something better than begging.

This crippled man was a beggar. All his life he had been lame; he had been born lame—that is all he had known, a life made difficult by his twisted, inadequate body.

Was his mind crippled also? Perhaps so! Perhaps he had come to the place which he believed was all life had for him—to beg his daily bread until the day death claimed him.

He had developed a "begging" voice, a kind of piteous whine that would touch the hearts of those who went to the church to pray. He had developed the technique of getting money until it had become an art to extract money from people. He was a beggar!

That is the substance of the first act of this drama. A professional beggar asks money of two Christian disciples, at the door of the church. If we, however, skip over the intervening acts and go at once to the last act of this drama, we see the same man . . . the man born lame . . . walking, leaping, and praising God. The question is "WHAT MADE THE DIFFERENCE?"

If you do not know the story, you will feel like asking, "Did some

famous bone specialist treat that man and so correct his deformity?"
or "Did some bright shining angel from the courts of glory touch that
man on his crippled, deformed body and so suddenly heal him?"

What made the difference? By what means did that man progress
from begging to praising, from stumbling about to walking and
leaping? What made the difference?

Let us see what happened when the beggar cried to Peter and John
for alms—money. The apostle Peter said to the beggar—looking
directly at him—"Look at us!" In other words, give us your attention!
If you want help, you must do something for yourself. We have
neither silver nor gold, but we have just received a great gift . . .
"LOOK AT US!"

I do not know what the beggar saw in the faces of Peter and John; I
do know that they had but recently been empowered with the Holy
Spirit. They had something which could not be hidden. They had
something which would not keep. Some things will keep—like stones
and diamonds. Some things can be pickled and preserved, but the real
things of life cannot be kept. Keep love and it will turn to lust. Keep
peace to your self and it will degenerate into passivity. Keep money
and it will corrupt your soul. Peter and John had something they
could not keep. They had something which had helped them, and
they believed it would help this beggar.

"LOOK AT US!" they told him. You are thinking about money
and what it will buy you; we want to tell you about something more
valuable. What we want to say to you will not reach your heart if your
mind is divided. Look at us!

Peter and John knew that the message they had for that beggar
would be more effective if he would look at them and see what effect
that same message had had in their lives.

This is always true. If what one sees in the life of a speaker who
urges you to go a certain way or to live or act in a certain way clashes
with the spirit of the content of his message, his words become
meaningless.

What you are and what you say must harmonize, or else your
message loses its impact. That is the secret of the persuasiveness of
Jesus.

In Him, the Word became flesh and dwelt among us. People
interpreted what they heard in terms of what they saw in His life.

So the early church preached the gospel, not so much in sermons, books, pamphlets, or lectures as in the enormous sacrifices and losses which they suffered in order to gain a convert and to witness to Christ.

It was Jesus and his life which inspired the early church and made them forget everything about themselves and sent them singing before the lion and the sword of persecution.

They could say to a doubting world: "LOOK AT US!" even as Peter and John said to that crippled beggar, "LOOK AT US." Can you say to the world, "Look at me!"? The beggar fixed his attention on them, expecting to receive something from them. To his surprise, Peter said to him, "I have no silver and gold, but I give you what I have; in the name of Jesus Christ of Nazareth, walk."

"And he [Peter] took him by the right hand [sinners need help] and raised him [the crippled man] up and immediately his feet and ankles were made strong. And leaping up he stood and walked and entered the temple with them, walking and leaping and praising God."

WHAT MADE THE DIFFERENCE?

By what means did that crippled beggar progress from begging to praising? He was no longer begging but praising. Between the two there is a great gulf. The gulf must be crossed if religion is to be a reality or a growing experience.

What made the difference? It was faith! They believed what Jesus had promised. "These signs," said Jesus, "will accompany those who believe: in my name they will cast out demons; they will speak in new tongues" (Mark 16:17, RSV). "Whatever you ask in my name, I will do it" (John 14:13, RSV). He said, also: "Whatever you ask the Father in my name, he may give it to you" (John 15:16, RSV). Peter and John believed the promises of Christ and they acted upon their belief. That is faith—belief put into act.

Their faith made the difference.

It is also true that the faith of the crippled beggar helped make the difference. "Get up and walk," said Peter, and immediately healing took place, and the man leaped to his feet.

His faith made the difference. Not his race, not his cultural level, not his educational background, not his social status—but his faith made the difference.

We live in a mechanical-type age; we are accustomed to pushing buttons and things work. But God cannot be moved by pushing buttons. Faith is the answer.

Ask that woman who had been troubled for years with a constant drain of blood from her system, leaving her weak, anemic, almost helpless. Ask her what made the difference. She will tell you that one day she decided that having tried all else she would try to contact the man called Jesus. But she saw that he was so surrounded with people it would be impossible for her to get to speaking nearness with him. She then decided, "If I may but touch his garment, I shall be whole" (Matthew 9:21). She did touch him and was healed. She would tell you, FAITH MADE THE DIFFERENCE.

Ask that Canaanite woman who came to Jesus, crying, "Have mercy on me, O Lord, thou Son of David, my daughter is grievously vexed with a devil." She is the woman to whom Jesus said, "It is not meet to take the children's bread, and to cast it to dogs." And she answered, "Truth, Lord, yet the dogs eat of the crumbs which fall from their masters' table." And to that Jesus replied, "O woman, great is thy faith: be it unto thee even as thou wilt" (Matthew 15:22, 26, 27, 28). She would tell you, FAITH MAKES THE DIFFERENCE.

Or ask those two blind men sitting on the roadside, crying to Jesus, "Have mercy on us, O Lord, thou Son of David." "What will ye that I shall do unto you?" asked Jesus, and they replied, "Lord, that our eyes may be opened" (Matthew 20:30, 32, 33). And their eyes were opened. They would tell you, FAITH MAKES THE DIFFERENCE.

Paul tells us in his letter to the Hebrews that it was faith that made Abel offer to God a better sacrifice than Cain's. Through faith he won God's approval as a righteous man. It was faith that kept Enoch from dying. Instead he was taken up to God, and nobody could find him, because God had taken him up.

It was faith that made Noah hear God's warning about things in the future that he could not see. He obeyed and built an ark in which he and his family were saved.

It was faith that made Abraham obey when God called him to go out into a country which God had promised him, leaving his own country without knowing where he was going.

It was faith that made Abraham offer his son Isaac as a sacrifice when God put Abraham to the test. It was faith that enabled the Israelites to cross the Red Sea as if on dry land. When the Egyptians tried to do it, the water swallowed them up.

It was through faith that many died under torture, refusing to accept freedom. Some were mocked and whipped, and others imprisoned.

It was faith that made the difference.

Faith makes the difference between begging and praising, between crawling and leaping.

No wonder the poet asked for:

> . . . a faith that will not shrink,
> Tho' pressed by ev'ry foe,
> That will not tremble on the brink
> Of any earthly woe.[1]

Are you troubled in mind? Faith is the answer!

Are you burdened with sorrow? Faith is the answer!

Are you crippled—lame—because of some sin? Faith is the answer!

---

[1] William H. Bathurst, "O for a Faith That Will Not Shrink," in A. M. Townsend, *The Baptist Standard Hymnal* (Nashville: Sunday School Publishing Board, 1924), p. 359.

The Lord Is
on Our Side

Dwight Clinton Jones

Now there arose up a new king over Egypt, which knew not Joseph (Exodus 1:8).

I remember as a child riding to church every Sunday morning with my family, and as we neared the church, a program would come on the air featuring a church in North Philadelphia. This church was somewhat unusual. It was active in gaining employment for its members and working in the community long before that type of thing was considered orthodox for the church. I remember that I would dread hearing the shrill soprano voice of what must have been a large black woman singing that church's theme song every Sunday—I can hear it today, "The Lord Is on Our Side, Emmanuel." The words never registered because the woman's voice was so unpleasant, but now the words fall upon my experience with new meaning.

Dwight Clinton Jones is pastor of the First Baptist Church of South Richmond, Virginia, having served as pastor of the Westwood Baptist Church of Richmond previously. He serves on the Board of Directors of many religious and civic organizations and is co-host of a weekly TV program, "Focus on Black Religious Life."

Surely a few years of living, a setback or two, a stark realization that the world is tough and life is difficult allow all of us to welcome soothing words that say "The Lord Is on Our Side, Emmanuel."

This sincere but untalented sister had not stumbled upon an idea that was new, for God's concern for the downtrodden has been evidenced ever since God cursed Cain for killing Abel.

The Israelites in the shadow of that massive Egyptian dynasty that saw them as little else than slave labor, the Jews being annihilated by the Germans, black folks under the foot of an accepted system of dehumanization—all felt that they could sing with this woman "The Lord Is on My Side, Emmanuel."

As if the oppression were not heavy enough; as if the back-breaking burden were not demeaning enough; as if folks having their own way with our women and children were not enough—slaves could and would still find heart to sing about a "Balm in Gilead that heals a sinsick soul." "Sometimes I feel discouraged and think my work is in vain, but then the Holy Spirit revives my soul again." "I'm a rolling through our unfriendly world." Yes, the chains of the physical and visible oppression are weighing us down, but—"The Lord Is on Our Side."

Jesus further substantiates the premise by consorting with harlots, calling publicans from trees and putting his feet under their tables, dealing with people on the basis of need, ignoring their station in life. The Lord Is on Our Side! "Amen!" shouts that woman, who bled for twelve years. "Right On!" cries that nobody by the pool for thirty-eight years. "I know what you're talking about," affirms that Samaritan woman by Jacob's well.

When nobody else would listen—spend some time—lift a helping hand—the Lord was on our side.

I hear some in this congregation today telling these saints, "Move over, for we too can attest the cognizance of a God who has been for us."

Those who don't feel particularly oppressed—those who have transcended the pit of the socioeconomic barrel—immediately cry out, "What kind of God is this? Doesn't he care for everybody?"

Perhaps the words of the Nazarene carpenter magnify the concept best—"It is easier for a camel to go through the eye of a needle, than for a rich man to enter into the kingdom of God" (Matthew 19:24).

God is not against the rich—he didn't say it would be an impossibility, just a difficult task. The more we receive, the harder it is to remember the benefactor. It is evident and apparent that some are so well off that they have gone off—to their own world that revolves not around the Son of God. "Whosoever doth not bear his cross and come after me cannot be my disciple," says Jesus. (See Luke 14:27.) God is not against the rich, but we know him as the Champion of the defenseless, the widow, the orphan, the powerless, and the poor. It is in this context that we are better able to see the Hebrew people on their journey. They had been in Egypt for 430 years, aliens in a pagan land, dependent upon the pleasure of Pharaoh for their peace and prosperity. Joseph had kept the equilibrium. Why, he was the Israelites' man in government—the Andy Young of that day, if you please. He had risen in the ranks of the Egyptian hierarchy after having been sold into slavery by his own flesh and blood. He was the interpreter of dreams who kept the Pharaoh on the right track. He ran interference for his people and kept their interest before the Pharaoh.

But Joseph died, and now there rose a king that knew not Joseph. This Pharaoh didn't know that Joseph had forecast that in the midst of trying times Egypt would prosper if they stored up resources during the seven years of plenty even though seven years of famine were to come. This Pharaoh didn't know Joseph had been the armor bearer for his people. With the new Pharaoh came new policy—slave labor—sweat—hard work. So the Israelites were now to test again the premise that God is for us. They were to find out anew through war scares, desert treks, and through watery paths that, yes—even though there is a new king on the throne—one who doesn't seem concerned about their rich history—one who doesn't seem concerned about their noble contributions—one who doesn't seem concerned about divine election by God—even though this king doesn't know Joseph—*God is on our side.*

This new king, in forgetting Joseph and the people Joseph represented so well, allowed his ego and his insecurity to drown out his concern for humankind and his sense of justice.

Pharaoh felt no need to be compassionate to these people; why, he was Pharaoh! The Egyptian people believed him to be a descendant of God. He owned everything and laid claim to everybody. Why, the great pyramids of Egypt were built so that the kings' bodies could be preserved with their souls which they felt would live on forever.

Pharaoh was Pharaoh. Why should he rule with a sense of justice? So often success, leadership, position, and power trot hand in hand with insensitivity and a rhinoceros skin when it comes to remembering where we come from.

History is pregnant with insensitive rulers who in a sense forgot Joseph and ruled as if yesterday were nonexistent and as if tomorrow would never come. Marie Antoinette, the beautiful queen of France who died at the guillotine, forgot that her power was with the people. Upon asking a court attendant why the people of Paris were angry, he replied, "They have no bread," and she reportedly retorted, "Let them eat cake."

Richard Nixon forgot the electorate and became enamored with the presidency. He told David Frost, "When the President does it, it means it's now legal"—or the president is above the law.

Self-made men and women, comfortable in their hard-earned security, say of the poor and uncared for, "Let them pull themselves up by their own bootstraps; that's how I made it."

Surely that's how many make it; that's how I made it; but lest we forget, I must remind you and myself also that even though we pulled, there was somebody pulling with us and for us. Lest we forget and become like Marie Antoinette, or begin to play god like a Nixon, we couldn't pull ourselves up without the aid and prayers of unseen persons who remembered to keep our names on the altar.

I sometimes get to feeling good about my journey when I think about the three jobs I worked in college—a cashier, a janitor, and a bank clerk. I begin to feel self-made and that I shaped my destiny. That by my power and might—that by my sweat and endurance I am here today—but I can't stand here like Pharaoh and forget what Joseph represents, nor can you, for I've got to remember godly parents and grandparents who, even though they had little or no money, encouraged me with words, prayer, and meager support.

I've got to remember those country churches that opened their pulpits and said, "Come, let's help each other."

I've got to remember those mentors along the way who weren't too busy to give a word of advice and cheer.

There rose a king who didn't know Joseph.

But, Pharaoh, you ought to find out about this man who served in your predecessor's cabinet, this man who interpreted dreams that made it possible for your mother and father to live through the famine. You ought to remember Joseph.

And likewise we ought not forget Joseph. Don't forget this giant of yesteryear whose contributions provided the footing and the tone for our pilgrimage through life.

Alex Haley, though generations removed, couldn't forget Kunte Kinte's yearning for freedom that had been placed in the breast of each succeeding generation.

Don't forget the stalwart personalities who lived and died that we might be free.

Don't forget Joseph—that relative who cared when no one else would.

Don't forget Joseph, that teacher who took an extra minute and gave you that extra shove.

Don't forget that church that gave you a meaningful philosophy of life and introduced you to Jesus Christ who is Emmanuel, which interpreted means "God with us."

Don't forget the prayers that were raised in your behalf when you were too foolish to pray for yourselves. Somebody had your name at the footstool of mercy. Somebody was praying that you would return to the Lord.

Don't forget where you came from—you'll appreciate it more when you do remember.

Don't forget who you used to be—you'll better understand those who are still trying to make it.

Don't forget your past weakness—you'll better understand your brother's present faults.

Don't forget the trials and troubles of yesterday.

If you don't forget Joseph—you will be able to affirm that God is on our side.

And so the insensitive Pharaoh who forgot Joseph gave us another case of few calling the many to lash. Pharaoh was fearful because the Israelites were multiplying so quickly. His fear was that a nation would rise up, and just as he had forgotten Joseph, they would forget Pharaoh. He feared that the minority would become the majority, and he would lose power. This has been the repetitous history of humankind. Those who have try to keep it away from those who have not.

But there will always be a voice—there will always be a movement—there will always be a minority report. The report that says even though the great and the numerous have spoken, there is another word from the few. And from this minority right and righteousness will always emerge victorious.

We don't have to look to Nazi Germany for an example. Nor do we have to look to South Africa where the physical minority with its vexed spirit and ill-fated rule over the majority has kept that people in bondage. Right here in America we know from personal treatment which we have received from the majority. Not until it appeared that our numbers would make a difference did politicians seek our counsel and answer our petitions.

And there is little difference in our ecclesiastical fortresses. There are always a few with made-up minds—consecrated spirits—their shoulders to the wheel.
A few who don't care if the work is rough—
A few who don't care if the deeds are difficult—
A few who try to keep the masses on the mark—
A few who tell us, "Seek ye first the kingdom of God"—
A few who tell us, "But God is not deceived, nor is he mocked"—
A few who try to keep us on target by telling us that we must keep our devotional life intact, our stewardship commitment current, our Bible study life active, and our worship life filled with the Holy Spirit. Always there are a few examples of those who have right priorities and made-up minds. A few folks with their minds stayed on Jesus can turn a lot of people around. Jesus started with twelve and one of them betrayed him. Most of our churches started in someone's house, just a few people.
Well, the minority rose up in Egypt.
They didn't have much—
Poverty-stricken—no money—
Memories—precious memories
An excuse for a leader—stammering tongue—indecisive spirit—
But they did have God on their side.
For God had promised Abraham before them,
"I shall make you a mighty nation

You will be my people, and I will be your God."
They didn't have much—but they did have a rich prayer life—
The will to make a change—they had a God who was on their side.
They did have the reassuring knowledge that if God is for you, he is
more than the world against you.
Yes, God is for us, and God is with us. With a support system like this
our rationalization for weakness takes on no meaning.

> "Let us, then, be up and doing,
> With a heart for any fate;
> Still achieving, still pursuing;
> Learn to labor and to wait."[1]

[1] Henry Wadsworth Longfellow, "A Psalm of Life."

Our Sure Defense

Dearing E. King

The Lord hath made bare his holy arm in the eyes of all the nations; and all the ends of the earth shall see the salvation of our God (Isaiah 52:10).

These divinely inspired words of the prophet Isaiah were addressed to Israel in exile. God's Chosen People had been taken into Babylonian captivity. Their miraculous adventure that was begun at Sinai had come to an inglorious end. As a matter of fact, Babylon was far worse than Egypt. In Egypt, for 430 years, they managed to maintain contact with Jehovah. But in Babylon they expressed their feeling of ultimate extinction: "Our bones are dried, and our hope is lost: we are cut off for our parts" (Ezekiel 37:11). In that strange land they not only felt cut off from their homeland but also from Jehovah himself. The atrocities which they suffered and the despair and fear

Dearing E. King is the former pastor of the Zion Baptist Church, Louisville, Kentucky, and Friendship Baptist Church, New York. Presently he is the pastor of Monumental Baptist Church, Chicago, Illinois.

Dr. King is well known as an American Baptist and Progressive Baptist pastor, writer, and lecturer.

which gripped them left these exiles without even a singing faith.

Now you can understand what the inspired words of the text meant to these terrified rejects. The prophet brings into clear view the sovereign posture of the everlasting Father in defense of his children of every land and clime unto the ends of the earth. "The Lord hath made bare his holy arm in the eyes of all the nations." His eternal concern for the downtrodden renders all at *one* with himself. Therefore, anyone who bucks him will encounter his fury. For he rolls up his sleeves in rageful defense of his people, while nations look on in horror, wonder, and awe. This explains the Lord's wrathful action against oppression anywhere and anytime.

Let us begin with the divine purpose for mankind. That purpose is justice and freedom for all peoples. Regardless of what place on the globe or the peoples involved, God's purpose of justice and freedom is timelessly relevant and current. No greater thought can be imagined, outside the reality of God himself, than for people to become convinced of God's purpose of justice and freedom for their lives. This thought is the bedrock of the Constitution of the United States of America—"Liberty and justice for all." The nation's intention is there, at least, on paper, if not in practice.

Today, as never before, the nobodies from nowhere are giving vigorous expression to this conviction. To deny justice and freedom to anyone is to deny them to all. Then one day we will wake up without them at all.

God has made each individual unique and distinct. Yet the very structure of human personality is laced with justice and freedom. Thus, when these divinely inherent rights are violated, God rolls up his sleeves and makes ready his holy arm for battle in defense of the least of his little ones.

Consider now the appointive means by which God's purpose is to be realized. For the general good of humanity, people must be governed. Otherwise there would be intolerable anarchy. Therefore, within the creative process is a governing principle. By virtue of this principle the Lord has brought into being governing bodies for the purpose of helping him to achieve justice and freedom. These are what the apostle Paul refers to when he says: "The powers that be are ordained of God. . . . For rulers are not a terror to good works, but to the evil" (Romans 13:1, 3). Hence, God's purpose is to be wrought out through governments, religious organizations, institutions, and agencies, all inspired by God. That is, God takes people and forms a compact with them to accomplish his purpose of justice and freedom.

But both rulers and the people must keep fully aware that these governments, religious organizations, institutions, and agencies are mere instruments. Hence, they must never attract attention to themselves. They should minister to the sacred cause as though everything depends on them. At the same time they must know that everything depends upon God.

In the divine purpose and cause there can be no exclusive place for nationalism, egoism, or even ecclesiasticism. Too much prominence of these ordained powers may obscure divine procedure and activity and thus render them unfit as means for which they were ordained. Therefore, all appointive means of evangelism, legislation, education, and social programs, etc., must be used for the purpose of helping God to achieve his goal of justice and freedom. Our failure to do so jeopardizes God's cause and brings his name into disrepute. Thus, he will rise up in righteous indignation and roll up his sleeves in wrathful action for all the world to see.

We conclude with God's personal intervention when nations and rulers fail to carry out his purpose of justice and freedom. Here his arm becomes redeemingly bare. You see, both history and experience give testimony to the truth that all nations conspire to violate the will, purpose, and even the mandate of God in assuring justice and freedom for all. When nations fail to use their power to help those in need, then God will personally take over in defense of the helpless and hopeless.

For instance, when Egypt held the Jews for 430 years in abject slavery and placed unbearable burdens upon them, God rolled up his sleeves and stepped down into the back of Jethro's pasture. He said to Moses: "I have surely seen the affliction of my people which are in Egypt. . . . And I am come down to deliver them out of the hand of the Egyptians . . ." (Exodus 3:7-8). The Lord rolled up his sleeves and wrecked Egypt and brought justice and freedom to his Chosen People. To this day Egypt has not fully recovered from the knockout.

Where is invincible Babylon that put the holy city of Jerusalem in ruins and destroyed the holy temple? Then she herded the Israelites, like cattle, to Babylon by the River Chebar. It was a ghetto that bred despair and death. In that strange land they were left without faith or freedom to sing. So deplorable were the conditions that God rolled up his sleeves and made bare his holy arm in the eyes of all the nations for all the ends of the earth to see. He knocked Babylon into oblivion, and she is still down, counted out.

This is what Calvary is all about. When man's redemption was at stake, God made bare his holy arm and came down in the likeness of his begotten Son. He even gave the world the advantage of arresting him, whipping him, spitting on him, and indicting him as a criminal. He allowed the combined powers of government and religion to strip him, nail him alive to a wooden cross. But even on the cross he made bare his holy arm, rolled up his sleeves, and proved that he could still win. With an almighty jab he smote the universe, and the blow was so tremendous that "the veil of the temple was rent in twain from the top to the bottom; and the earth did quake, and the rocks rent; and the graves were opened, and many bodies of the saints which slept arose" (Matthew 27:51-52). The centurion felt the blow and screamed, "Truly this was the Son of God" (Matthew 27:54).

On Easter Sunday morning Christ arose. He wrung the sting from death and shook the victory from the grave. Then in these words he declared himself the winner: "All power is given unto me in heaven and in earth" (Matthew 28:18).

Today America and the world had better come to terms with the two postures of the Son of God. He is the Lamb of God. But he is also the Lion of Judah. And he hath made bare his holy arm to destroy anything that gets in his way. As the title of a current play puts it: *Your Arm's Too Short to Box with God.* Or as Isaac Watts invites all the world to sing:

> "Under the shadow of thy throne
> Thy saints have dwelt secure;
> Sufficient is thine *arm* alone,
> And our defence is sure."

Yes, the Lord still reigns while nations rise and fall. With his holy arm made bare, "He shall not fail nor be discouraged, till he have set judgment in the earth . . ." (Isaiah 42:4). And we shall not fail him until we crown him Lord of all.

Women of Faith

Ella Pearson Mitchell

For ye are all the children of God by faith in Christ Jesus (Galatians 3:26).

This is certainly a good time to speak on "Women of Faith." Women are very big in the news, what with the first federally funded women's national conference recently held in Houston. The present first lady and the former first lady were there, along with many other great ladies. But perhaps the most striking news to come from Houston was the realization that there are women dedicated to *opposing* equal rights for women. There are *women* who believe that there are differences in the basic equality of human beings! It's like that miniscule minority of blacks over a century ago who opposed the abolition of slavery. Like that appalling handful who thought they were better off as slaves, these more numerous sisters seem to prefer

Ella Pearson Mitchell is a well-known American Baptist educator, lecturer, and churchwoman. She is a former president of the American Baptist Board of Education and Publication. Presently she is on the staff of the Ecumenical Center for Black Church Studies, Los Angeles.

She is the wife of Dr. Henry H. Mitchell, a renowned author, lecturer, and minister.

their pretty prisons. This indeed *is* news in our time!

Among the slaves who opposed abolition the problem was clearly a lack of faith. They feared the unknown and dreaded the prospect of dying in the uncharted wilderness of freedom, when they could die full in the Egypt of slavery. However, praise God, the vast majority sought freedom, regardless of their keen awareness of the dangers. By faith in Jesus Christ, they *knew* that they were children of God and destined to be free.

It is this same lack of faith which, in all likelihood, ails the women who oppose equal rights. The words of Paul in our text are spoken to persons like unto them. They deal with coming out from under another kind of slavery, a hard-to-shake traditional slavery to the Law. Paul says very clearly, "You are children of *God,* by faith in Jesus Christ"—princes and princesses of the Universe, if you are willing to claim or accept it by faith. But that had to be a two-directional kind of experience. The offer was good, yes: "Come, unto me all ye that labor and are heavy laden." There was no date when it would take effect and no expiration date either. It did not depend on the action of some august body, such as the Congress or the voting public or the president. The only way in which it was qualified was the requirement of the response of faith. No matter how good the offer of liberty and membership in the family of God, it is useless until accepted. Until you claim it by faith, you are still under the old yoke.

Two verses later, Paul says, "There is neither Jew nor Greek, there is neither bond nor free, there is neither male nor female: for ye are all one in Christ Jesus." Taking Paul quite literally, blacks are declared by faith to be no longer bound to masters in a cruel system of total exploitation. By faith, also, we are no longer slaves to the Jewish law, especially if we are Greeks in the first place. And by faith we women are no longer different and discriminated against—indeed no longer trapped in the narrow confines so carefully assigned us by an inhuman and unholy cultural bias.

If this seems a rather harsh and "sudden" statement to make about us women, especially in such solid biblical phrases, let me point out clearly that God has *always* used some women in very "high-powered" and visibly responsible positions.

One of the least known of these was a prophet by the name of Anna, who was in fact the first person of all to declare that Jesus would become the Christ, the Savior of the world. Anna lived in the temple at Jerusalem; at a very ripe old age she was still a full-time staffer at the First Church of Jerusalem. If you've never heard of her, read about her in Luke 2:36-38. Find out more about her, for she is a pioneer of the faith!

Perhaps a better known woman in high places among the servants of God was Deborah—a prestigious judge in Israel. Chapters 4 and 5 of the Book of Judges mention this great political figure who was centuries ahead of her time but recognized both for her wise counsel and her abiding faith in God. Her faith was such that she could indeed be called a prophet. God permitted and indeed commanded this to be so *early* in the history of the faith.

I hardly need recall for you Queen Esther. She is remembered by us all for her courageous acts—not because she was a queen in the traditional sense of limited feminine scope, but because she took upon herself the liberation of her people from a deadly decree. She stepped out of the role of the demure queenie—the legally silenced female in the courts of law—and declared the famous words, "If I perish, I perish." And you remember, of course, that she saved her folk from racial genocide.

I think, also, of two women of faith who stand out in the ministry of Jesus. Both were women from outside the Jewish household of faith. One is the woman of the supposedly despised Samaritans, who met our Lord at a well in her country. Her story confirms the belief that God is no respecter of persons, and that Jesus is the Christ, the giver of the very *water of life!* Her witness to her hometown folks was, "Come, see a man . . .!" Yes, whatever her sins and her ignorance of spiritual things, Jesus placed her in position to be called the first evangelist.

The other woman who comes to mind was the Syro-Phoenician woman, weary and worn from the care of her stricken daughter. She was at the end of her rope when she went to plead with Jesus for her daughter. Earnestly she cried out, "Have mercy! Lord, *please* help me!" When Jesus tested her with a culturally stereotypical put-down of her race and sex, she pressed right on, humble in the extreme, but very tenacious. Her perseverance must have touched Jesus deeply, for that obstinate faith was rewarded with one of the greatest compliments Jesus ever gave anyone: "O woman, great is thy faith!"

(Matthew 15:28). Yes, God has always used some women to do the work of the kingdom, and from top to bottom of the echelons as the world sees them.

The thing we need to face is that God calls today—NOW—for all women to match the levels of faith of women like Anna and Deborah and Esther and the nameless others. God calls us to a life-style of full expression and usefulness, by faith. And this, my beloved, is no fluke—no bizarre challenge to the impossible. The hand of the Creator has evidence everywhere for us to see. For instance, tests have long since proven that women are the intellectual equals of men. Now quite obviously God did not give women all that intelligence to "clam up" and "play dumb." If indeed women do have a different *kind* of intelligence, then that feminine genius is precisely what we need in the world today. Masculine aggressiveness and warlike violence are about to destroy it.

But even if one wants to measure women by a rock 'em-sock 'em "hemale" standard, what greater heroine does America have than a black woman named Harriet Tubman? General Moses, if you please to call her that, returned to the South many, many times, and brought out hundreds of her slave brothers and sisters. Hers was the most daring and ingenius and the most disciplined technique of the entire Underground Railroad. And yet, again, it must be understood that Harriet Tubman was a woman whose fantastic courage was based on faith. Nothing but faith could give anybody the idea that she could go into the very jaws of hell as often as she did and bring out her beloved unscathed. Only by faith did she know God, and that her God would make a way. The magnitude of her faith is astounding, for no other person in all American history has overcome her military and operational disadvantages.

Many will still argue that to free women as much as the Word decrees is "awful risky." A few token women, yes, but not all that earth-shaking change, at least not in such a hurry. The Bible has good examples, but they weren't in large numbers, and who would dare *try* to stand in Harriet Tubman's shoes? And who am I to deny that sweeping changes like this are risky? Yet I can only say that if, indeed, in Christ is neither male nor female, then there is no safer place than to stand in the middle of the will of God. Storms may rage and risks abound, but those who stand on the spot to which God has called them are always in a more blessed place than anyone else can claim. You needn't fritter away time figuring out how it will look to the rest of the people; if God has directed you to witness in your time, then God will make a way for you. If you have the faith to follow, no other questions need be asked.

All my life I have heard about a young lady who was called to a *very* risky place of witness—she was called indeed to be the mother of Jesus himself. When the angel spoke unto her, she found it very hard to deal with what she was called to do. Finally, by *faith,* she said, "Behold the handmaid—the servant—of the Lord. What*ever* God wants me to do, I'll do it. I don't understand it, and I have some fears about how people will see me, but I serve God by faith." So, by *faith,* became she the mother of the Savior of the world. And what the angel said to her was indeed true: "Hail, Mary, full of grace, *blessed* art thou—*happy* are you—fortunate are you, even in this risky vocation—richly recognized are you in that you have found favor with God and have responded to God's call in faith."

We are all children of God by faith in Christ Jesus, and in the host of the most faithful witnesses there is neither male nor female. They are the company of the new earth, the new Jerusalem, the very kingdom of God. The world has not yet learned to like them, but what does it matter to the very children of God?

The Wise Men

James N. Mitchell

(A Sermon for Advent)

Let me tell you two stories about "wise men."

One of the many Christmas stories which bears telling and retelling is one by William Locke, concerning three Englishmen, bachelors—learned professors who found themselves on a train one Christmas Eve—headed for the country estate of a casual acquaintance. Each of the three would much rather have been at home with his books in the quiet of his undisturbed surroundings.

After many stops and delays, due to extreme weather, the three finally arrived at a station, where they were met by a chauffeur with a private car. Soon he had them bundled into the car, and after some miles the gentlemen were almost beginning to enjoy themselves. Then, suddenly, there was a lurch and a jolt and the car came to a

James N. Mitchell, former chaplain, Toledo State Hospital, holds a B.S. degree from Morehouse College where he was a classmate of Martin L. King, Jr., the B.D. from Oberlin College, and the Th.D. from Vanderbilt University.

Dr. Mitchell directs the Youth Poverty Program for New York City and presently serves as a psychologist and consultant on youth and religion.

stop—with a broken axle. The only thing the chauffeur knew to do was to start walking the five miles to the nearest inn for help. He suggested that during the interval the three gentlemen might take shelter in a small house which they had passed about one-half mile back.

This they did. When the three grumbling men arrived in front of the house, one of them stumbled over a large object and found it to be a man lying in the snow—frozen. They carried him into the miserable little house; and as they entered, they heard an uncanny sound from one of the rooms. Upon investigation, they found a woman in childbirth—unconscious. The three learned men—each one renowned in his special field—looked at each other helplessly in the face of this most elemental of life's mysteries.

The next two hours were ones they would have liked to forget. They did things almost instinctively. As the fire they had built began to warm the small house, there was a cry of new life—and with that cry, the woman breathed her last. They placed the man gently beside his wife in the other room. And they wrapped the child in some of their warm clothing, salvaged from the stalled car. Then they laid the infant on an improvised bed of their fur coats. One of them looked at his watch and announced that it was Christmas morning; and another, almost in a trance, said, "Unto us a child is born. . . ."

Then it was that the child stirred and cried, and they were all on their knees to minister to it—and the scene had all the appearance of a modern "adoration."

Surely, while I have been telling this story in brief, your minds have been noting both similarities and differences between this modern story of three learned men and the Christmas story of the three wise men as we have it in Matthew's Gospel. In order that we might think further upon these similarities and differences, listen to a portion of the familiar Gospel account in the somewhat different wording of Phillip's translation:

> Jesus was born in Bethlehem, in Judaea, in the days when Herod was king of the province. After his birth, there came from the east a party of astrologers making for Jerusalem and enquiring as they went, "Where is the child born to be king of the Jews? For we saw his star in the east and we have come to pay homage to him."
>
> . . . And now the star, which they had seen in the east, went in front of

them until at last it shone immediately above the place where the little child lay. The sight of the star filled them with indescribable joy.

So they went into the house and saw the little child with his mother Mary. And they fell on their knees and worshipped him. Then they opened their treasures and presented him with gifts—gold, incense and myrrh (Matthew 2:1-2, 9-11, J. B. Phillips).

I want to say four things about the similarities and differences of these two stories.

The first is the obvious similarity of the wisdom and learning in each group of three men. They were wise in having studied much. This is an important element in each story. For we know that a knowledge of history and philosophy and astronomy and other sciences does add a dimension to human understanding that makes a difference. It makes a difference both in one's approach to a situation and one's response. Such is the case in these stories. Contrast the simple response of the shepherds on the hillside to that of the questioning, inquiring wise men, and you catch something of this. Put three hard-working peasants in place of the three learned Englishmen and the complications of the situation ease up a good deal. The fact of learning—this kind of wisdom—is important, and much the same, in each story.

The second comparison goes on beyond the fact of learning and wisdom to the immediate reason of why they were journeying. And this brings out a difference between the stories. The wise men were looking for the "King of the Jews"—they had a purpose and a goal which had meaning. They knew the prophecies concerning his coming; they knew the importance of this event for the Hebrew nation; and in the light of their understanding they, too, wanted to find him and pay homage to him. Theirs was a self-chosen purpose. But the modern wise men were journeying out of social pressure. They were going visiting because it was expected of them—because that's what people do on Christmas Eve. Each was wrapped up in his own interests, and that which happened on the journey was completely unwanted, unlooked for, and undreamed of. These three were thrust by circumstance into a meaningful experience.

This brings us to the third comparison—which is also a point of contrast in the two stories. The event in each case—the birth of a child—brought the men to their knees (both literally and figuratively), but for quite different reasons. The wise men who had known of the prophecies of a Messiah, and who had journeyed to find this new King, fell on their knees because they knew themselves to be in the presence of royalty. They offered gifts worthy of the greatness of a king. Outwardly, there was only a simple babe in simple surroundings, but there was—for those who understood—the promise of something greater implicit in their "adoration."

For our three modern wise men, the babe whom they had helped to welcome into this world received their homage simply because of his humanity and his helplessness. No kingly promises or experiences—only the overpowering demands of helpless humanity thrust into the hands of one who can help—this brought each man to his knees.

These two sets of learned men, then—who journeyed for quite different reasons—who knelt beside a babe for quite different reasons—have yet one more point of comparison—probably the most important one of all. In each story we are aware of the common element of human "greatness" being humbled in the presence of human "simplicity," or "reality." The men are utterly divested of the false dignity of learning or the earthly importance of wisdom. Their learning and wisdom are important only as they serve the needs of a small child, or the hopes for a Messiah; only as they prove that they can stand and grow in the face of the "common"; only as they stand the test of compassion.

Much of the power of the story of the Nativity lies in this contrast of the coming of the Deliverer—the King—in the form of a simple, helpless child. Regardless of how we look upon these birth stories in our Gospels, they ring true to our total Christian gospel because they are consistent with Jesus' whole life, death, and resurrection at this very point. Never did Jesus disdain human learning, as such, but consistently he turned to the sinners and the simple folk to convey his message. Again and again he insisted upon performing simple tasks in all simplicity. He stood before earthly rulers in marked contrast to their greatness—with simple bearing and words. He accepted death as a common criminal; and after his death, he appeared to only a few—those humble folk who had believed in him. Throughout the pages of the Gospel accounts we see human "greatness" humbled by his kind of simple "greatness."

How can these comparisons help us see ourselves as "wise men"?

These comparisons concerning two sets of wise men can help us see ourselves a bit more clearly, if we will. For whether we like it or not, we who live in this privileged land—who have had the opportunities for higher education—have much in common with these "wise men" about whom we have been talking.

We may envy the simple peasant or shepherd. With a wistfulness we may wish that we could go back to grasping truth through "angel singing" and the simple acceptance of the heart. But we cannot. We come to our understanding of the incarnation, as we come to every other great Christian truth, first with our minds. We know the setting, with all its desperate longings. We understand something of mankind's needs and hopes for a Savior—both then and now.

And this knowledge—this learning—rather than being a problem, can help us to a fuller experience of the Advent of Christ. And it will if we go on to the other matters of journeying, kneeling, and offering gifts.

Some of us can journey like those first wise men, with full awareness of the need for deliverance and of God's promise of a Deliverer. We can come ready to pay homage to a King, expectantly bringing him gifts. Others of us can do no more than those three modern wise men did. Like them, we can journey only out of response to others, or in response to something almost forgotten from our childhood. We move toward the event almost in spite of ourselves. But we do journey.

And having set out upon this journey, whatever our reasons, we can come to the experience of kneeling at the manger. We can be brought to our knees in humility as we stand before a newborn child. For there is always hope in a child. At the manger, this hope can be the tremendous hope of the incarnation, when the meaning of that event is grasped. Or it can be nothing more than the simple hope inherent in all human life. Both force us to kneel.

And having knelt, whatever our reasons, it is possible to experience the humbling which comes as we find ourselves in the presence of simple greatness. We need this! We need to kneel at the manger again and again and be stripped of all our learned pretensions—all our preoccupations of the mind—all our pride in our wisdom.

Here is an event to help us learn the necessity of using our learning for greater understanding of God and his ways. Here is an annual experience to help us test our wisdom by the simple greatness of Christ himself.

To know and to understand is not to doubt, but to comprehend more fully, the incarnation. May the wise men stand as reminders for us that the birth stories in the Gospels are true—true to all that we know of Christ and his "way"—true to all that he revealed of God and man and their relationship one to the other. This we know by the coming together of our minds and our hearts in one experience of adoration—wise men, kneeling at a manger.

This experience is not only history but also hope for each of us today, in a time when we need it so badly! Of course this manger of old is gone with the winds and rains of centuries, but the Christ of redemption is still among us, waiting for us to come before him in deep humility and adoration.

We need this humbling experience. We need this divine encounter with our Redeemer. We need to abide in the presence of the Almighty so that we may rise up from our knees and go into the world and tell men that there is hope!

As the poets said:

> "Earth has no sorrow that heaven cannot heal!"[1]

> "Prayerful souls may find Him by our quiet lakes,
> Meet Him on our hillsides
> Where the morning breaks.
> In our fertile cornfields
> While the sheaves bound,
> In our busy markets,
> Jesus may be found."[2]

[1] Thomas Moore and Thomas Hastings, "Come, Ye Disconsolate."
[2] J. T. East, "Wise Men Seeking Jesus."

Nobody Knows
Our Names

John R. Porter

The man gave names to all cattle, and to the birds of the air, and to every beast of the field. . ." (Genesis 2:20*a*, *The Common Bible*).

Now when Jesus came into the district of Caesarea Philippi, he asked his disciples, "Who do men say that the Son of man is?" (Matthew 16:13, RSV).

The creation story in the book of Genesis opens with God creating the world, naming things, and naming people. Then the Scripture states that God gave man, Adam, the power to name things. The meaning of this text seems clear: "The man gave names to all cattle, and to the birds of the air, and to every beast of the field."

You will note that as God created and named man and named everything, he declared that it was "good." How good was God

John R. Porter is a renowned scholar and a former United Methodist Pastor. In 1975 he received the Ph.D. degree from Union Graduate School, Yellow Springs, Ohio. He is also a graduate of Garrett Evangelical Theological Seminary, where he is an adjunct professor. He holds a B.A. from Iowa Wesleyan College. Presently he is the vice-president of Urban Affairs, Young Life Campaign.

in these acts? So good that he conferred the power of naming upon man. Imagine that! God is so good toward us that he gave us the power to name ourselves as well as things around us. In giving us dominion and power over things, God only required that we not profane this power to name and control people and things. Let us for a moment examine this God-given power to name people and things.

To have a name, to be named, to name people and things is to possess dominion and power over people and things. It is the naming of himself and things around him which brings spatial and territorial power to man. God has not created any people anywhere without this power of naming themselves and things around them. Names reflect an identity, a place in time and space, a heritage, a territory, possessions, boundaries, and laws. Names also mean rootage in some religious or metaphysical system or some mythological system which extends us into the past and projects us into the future. Our languages and symbols represent guides and maps into the private and public world of naming. It is the Spirit of God which motivates us to name ourselves and our world. We must name our children, our enemies, our cities, towns, streets, events, heroes, institutions, etc. New York, Chicago, London, Moscow, Tokyo, Nairobi, and Hong Kong—all represent the naming of powerful places where millions of people live. That is why the text says ". . . the man gave names to all. . . ."

Our ancient African ancestors believed that a child's name is related to both the child's behavior and its personality. Many African parents still wait a few days or a few weeks to name a newborn baby. Why? Life is viewed as an organic whole; that is, life is composed of the community of the living, dead, and unborn. If the good spirit of some long-deceased ancestor was observed as dominant in part of the baby's personality, then naming the child after that good ancestor meant continuing the line of goodness all the way back to God himself. Of course, no society, African societies included, has been able to prevent evil from showing up. The beauty of our African ancestors' naming rituals was their recognition that just to invent any old name for a child might well mean inviting a host of unnecessary evil spirits into the child's character. For example, very few parents would name their child "Satan" or "Lucifer." You can probably count the mothers on one hand who have named their daughters "Jezebel."

In both biblical and African societies everybody knew his name. That is to say, there was an unbroken generational link all the way back to those first ancestors. It was not unusual in these societies for people to recite orally more than twenty generations (six hundred years or more) of ancestral history.

"... I am the son/daughter of so-and-so, who was the father of so-and-so, who was the father of so-and-so, who was the father of so-and-so. ..."

But the God of our fathers' fathers does not want us wandering around in the long past of our biblical or African ancestors. While some of us will name our children Shem, Japheth, Meshech, Ashkenaz, or Arpadhshad, we are more prone to name our children John—because we want them to "walk in Jerusalem just like John"; Esther—because we want our girls to be queens who will not sell out the group; Paul—because we believe that God has a radical plan for the saving of his people. We would never name our children Judas because we know Judas "tommed" for the Romans.

This business of naming and identity bothers the conscientious black person living in America today. It is as if nobody knows our names. One writer, James Baldwin, wrote a book during the 1960s called *Nobody Knows My Name*. Another writer, Ralph Ellison, wrote a book during the 1940s entitled, *The Invisible Man*. And still another brother, Alex Haley, spent twelve years writing the most definitive book on black existence in the world—a book about black people because they were convinced that "nobody knows our names." We were shocked and angry when the late honorable Elijah Muhammad told us that the names we are wearing belonged to the slave master. What really rankled us was when he told us that white folks gave us their names so that they could maintain psychological control over us. Some of us cussed the Muslims under breath, but we knew deep down that they had touched upon a most vulnerable point of anger—the realization that somebody had prevented us from naming ourselves. And there was the subtle hint by Malcolm X that the blind acceptance of our present names had a lot to do with our divisiveness, backbiting, mimicking of white folks, self-contempt, general frustration, hypertension, and mental illnesses.

Then the truth began to tumble out. Gilbert Osofsky has touched on this matter of naming. Osofsky tells us:

When Muslims today relinquish their "given" names and search for others or replace them with an X, they touch upon one of the most debasing consequences of slavery—the denial of human dignity. The right to have or choose one's own name is the right to be; the power to control a man's name is authority to subjugate the man himself. Most slaves seem to have been given Christian names of a Biblical nature, but some were ridiculed or burlesqued from birth with such labels as Bashful, Virtue, Frolic, Gamesome, Lady, Madame, Duchess, Cowslip, Spring, Summer, Caesar, Pompey, Strumpet, and so on. Nothing better reveals the derisive nature of slavery than the act of naming.[1]

Most slaves who maintained some sort of sanity or faith wanted three or four definite changes when they were freed. First, they were determined to get themselves a new name; second, they wanted to learn to read, especially the Bible, and write, they wanted to live in a decent house and wear decent clothes, and they wanted to get married in the right way—before a preacher. In addition, it is recorded that many slaves wanted to exercise control over the rearing of their children.

In reaction to this sort of history and the deadening effect it has had upon the consciousness of many blacks, a number of well-known blacks have resorted to adopting Arabic and African names to replace the Western names. Thus, Lu Alcindor is now Kareem Abdul Jabbar; Cassius Clay is Muhammad Ali; Leroi Jones is now Imamu Amiri Baraka; and Don L. Lee is now Haki Madhubuti.

What these men are saying is that "nobody knows our names." They are saying that their present names grant too much psychological power to whites over blacks. There is a theological paradox here which these men have not entirely resolved by adopting non-European names. Some slaves felt that they had psychologically and spiritually transcended the categorical imperatives of the white man's power by adopting biblical names related to the prophets and the apostles. There is still the question in the average person's mind of why a man of Kareem Abdul Jabbar's wealth and prestige would not be satisfied until he also had the power to control the renaming of himself. While Kareem and other wealthy athletes may have answered this question of naming for themselves, it is questionable whether they have answered it for millions of other blacks.

[1] Quoted in Gilbert Osofsky, *Burden of Race* (New York: Harper & Row, Publishers, 1967), p. 32.

When some black person talks about how "tough" Einstein was, how "tough" the American system is, how "tough" his new "ride" is, then, we may be dealing with a person who has a false sense of inadequacy. Worse, he may be experiencing this namelessness I've been talking about. Such a man does not consider naming the great rivers in order to convert their mighty powers into electrical energy; he does not consider naming and capturing some of the power of the four winds in order to cause it to transport him across land and sea; he does not consider naming and controlling land in order to grow and market food for the world; he does not consider consulting the spirits in nature in order to discover cures for diseases like cancer and hypertension; he does not consider going to the namer of names and things in order to "know his name." He has not been confronted by Jesus at a deep enough level.

And if we are finally to get way, way, way back to our names—if we are truly to know our names, we must get acquainted with the name which is above every name. The name of Jesus connects us to God in a direct way. The theological profundities of the slave ancestors make this connection in the song: "I told Jesus it would be alright if he changed my name." Or, in the words of the great gospel singer, Rev. Cleophus Robinson,

> When he calls me, I will answer.
> I'll be somewhere listening for my name.
> Oh, I'll be somewhere listening for my name.

If I am lost from my name, from my roots, estranged from my being, from my God, Jesus promises to lead me all the way back. If anybody knows my name, Jesus has promised to give me a new name. If slave masters have hung the wrong name on me, he has promised to straighten it out. If the ox and the mule know how to respond to their master, I ought to be able to respond to the offer of Jesus. If the house dog and house cat know how to respond to their master's call, then I should easily recognize my master's voice; if the caged bird knows how to respond to its master's call, then I ought to be able to cry out: "I love the Lord; he's heard my cry." Who do men say that we are? Well, men have called us many things. We have been lied about, stolen, treated like everything but children of God. The world does not know our names. The world has called us boys when we were men. The world has called us colored when we desired to be black; the world has called us niggers when there is no nigger land; the world has been backwards on the evolutionary scale when Leakey says that we were first on the evolutionary scale; the world has tried to make us invisible, but some say that "we sing songs that not even the angels are able to sing"; the world has tried to act as though we had no theological basis for our existence, but now our theological experiences may represent salvation for the world; and, it is because of this that we might be wise to change that great old spiritual of "Nobody Knows the Trouble I See," to:

> Nobody knows the names I've carried.
> Nobody knows but Jesus.
> Sometimes my name's been up,
> Sometimes my name's been down. Oh, yes, Lord.

In a speech Andrew Young of Atlanta (now Ambassador to the United Nations) analyzed the change in the South's attitude toward blacks who now have the vote:

> Used to be all you could hear in the South was "nigguh this and nigguh that." As Blackfolk gained a little more political power, Southern politicians started saying "Negroes." Now that we have several million new Black voters in the South, it is amazing how fast those who yesterday could only say "Nigguh" and "nigras," now say with the greatest of ease, "Black people!"

Being nameless or possessing a bad name can exist for the educated as well as the uneducated. One can have a Ph.D. and be as nameless as a rock or dead tree. To be without a name is to be without historical roots, without a heritage, without power, without a cause, without a purpose, without a spirit, without a soul, without the One who names people and all things. One generation used to warn us that "you've got to know where you've come from in order to know where you're going." That's like saying "you've got to know who you are in order to know your purpose in the world."

Let us look back for a moment at some of our nameless ancestors—who, though nameless, yet possessed names which were invisible to those who had misnamed them. They held onto names from heaven because they believed that "God had the power to put His Spirit into the angels who cannot sing." They were talking about a power which

caused great musical visions to spring from their souls. They were
faithful products of a religious heritage similar to that of an old slave
preacher who lived close to the Source of life. On Sundays it was the
custom of this particular plantation to allow its slaves to worship with
the white folks—but the slaves had to come in after white people and
sit in the back. As the story goes, the old preacher would say to each
one as he filed out of church behind whites:

> "When y'all finish yo chores, come on down in the woods yonder wheres
> we can meet the Lord. Y'all ain't met Him in there. Come on down where
> you can hear the Lord call yo name."

When they finished their chores, they would sneak off one by one
and gather at the feet of the old preacher, gather to hear God call their
names. Having been called everything but a child of God, they needed
to hear their names called. Everybody needs to hear his name called
once in a while. Paul says that one day there will be a sound like a
mighty trumpet and that even those who died shall appear at the
calling of their names. As they stood and sat around, the old preacher
caused shouting, dancing, and great joy to stream from their souls as
he told them:

> "Brothers and sisters, y'all ain't no slaves. God ain't got no slavery up in
> heaven. Y'all ain't no nigguhs. God ain't got no nigguhs in heaven. Y'all
> ain't all them names they give us either. Children . . . children! Children!
> Do you know who you are? You the greatest thing God put here. You
> God's Children. God gave you a name just like he gave you a song to sing.
> So sing yo song and walk with yo head up high . . . cause one day when the
> Roll's called up yonder, y'all going to be the first names he calls."

No, I am not invisible and somebody knows my name. He knows
my name. I was here from the beginning. I was here when Eden was
formed. I was here before the great oceans received their names. I was
here when the first bird sang its first song. I was here before the great
beasts of the jungle received their names. I was here before the moon
and stars took their places in the galaxies. I was here when Adam
rebelled against God. I was here when Cain slew his brother Abel. I
was there when Jacob stole Esau's birthright. I was there when the
great prophets said, "Thus, saith the Lord, thou shall not serve false
gods." I was there when Ezekiel prophesied to the dry bones. I was
there when Amos cried for "justice to roll down like waters, and

righteousness like a mighty stream." I was there when Daniel stood the test of hungry lions. I was there when Jesus put that profound question to us: "Who do you say I am?" I was there when Peter answered: "The Christ, the Messiah, the Son of the living God." I was there when he told Peter that only God could reveal this name to him.

Somebody has said of Jesus, "He's the man nobody knows." Somebody needs to say, "He is the man evil men try hard not to know and good men ought to do all they can to know." Jesus—he's the man for all seasons. When they took him to court, nobody knew his name either. Pilate washed his hands and denied him. The fickle masses whom he fed and healed were afraid to identify with him. Peter denied him three times. His disciples ran away scared. Nobody knew his name. His friends didn't want to know him. His enemies didn't care to know him. But he knew us and he loved us to the end. Even as the last earthly breath oozed from his physical body, he thought enough of us to say: "Father, forgive them, for they know not what they do."

Jesus knew who he was, but we do not know who we are. Think about that! God knows each of us. John tells us that if we come to know God, he will give us the power to become his sons and daughters. If I'm his son, then I have his name. If I'm his son, then I have a place. If I'm his son, then I have a purpose. If I'm his son, then I've got a home economic system that Marxism, capitalism, or racism cannot take away. If I'm his son, I know that I have an inheritance—I know that one day I'll inherit his name and all that he stands for. If I'm his son, then, when he calls me, I'll answer. If I'm his son, then one day I am destined to fly away with him. If I'm his son, I must take him at his word when he tells me: "If I . . . if I be lifted up, I'll draw all men unto me."

Because I'll be somewhere listening for my name. When he calls me, I'll be somewhere listening for my name. When he calls, where, oh, where will you be? When he calls your name—so loud that it'll wake up the dead—where, oh, where will you be? When he calls you, will you answer?

A Nation Under God

Samuel D. Proctor

Stand fast therefore in the liberty wherewith Christ hath made us free . . .(Galatians 5:1).

We have been proud and grateful in our celebration of the nation's two hundred years of independence. We celebrated not only our liberation from the oppression of George III, but also more importantly we celebrated the founding of the *greatest political experiment* that men have ever devised. Samuel Adams wrote to a friend, during those early days, that *no* group of men, in *any* age had enjoyed the privilege of sitting down at a table, looking over all of the plans of governments, and choosing one that they believed to be best. No other men had ever had that privilege.

Samuel D. Proctor is pastor, professor, and preacher. Dr. Proctor has many distinctions, among them former President of Virginia Union University, President of North Carolina A. T. College, Director of the Peace Corps, and pastor of Congdon Street Baptist Church, Providence, Rhode Island.

Dr. Proctor presently is pastor of the historical Abyssinian Baptist Church, New York, succeeding the late Congressman Rev. Adam Clayton Powell. Also he is a professor of religion at Rutgers University.

Our founding fathers, sitting in Philadelphia, two hundred years ago, just reached back across the centuries and selected the most sublime, the most coherent, the most practical, rational, and elegant ideas that had ever possessed the mind of man. They began with the timeless idea in the Judaic-Christian tradition that we all had *one* great Creator, who made of one blood all nations to dwell on the face of the earth. They looked to the prophets in Jerusalem and to the scholars of Athens; they borrowed from the Roman law of Augustus Caesar and the sense of charity and vocation found in the Christian church; they picked up the accent on man and his genius that flowered in the Renaissance; they lifted individual liberty out of the Reformation and political self-determination out of John Locke and the Enlightenment.

So, America, in addition to an abundance of rich soil, with deep, clean rivers flowing like crystal between her majestic mountains, her magic climate, her rhythmic seasons and rainfall, her long shorelines, protected by expansive and boundless seas, and with trusted neighbors, north and south—with all of these endowments she then has the further blessing of the richest heritage of *ideas* that any people were ever bequeathed.

We ought to be extremely grateful as a people, having the most perfect system of government, based on the distilled fragrance of the best ideas men have ever conceived.

And with these monumental endowments the founding fathers brought the original thirteen colonies into one nation, the United States of America. It was *not* perfect. Not everyone who came over on the *Mayflower* was a paragon of virtue. Some colonies were made of paupers and vagabonds, brought here to get them out of the mother country. And the institution of slavery was an awful indictment of men who clamored for their own freedom. However, *with* these imperfections and limitations the colonists sprang free from the tyranny of Great Britain and brought a new nation into being.

But political liberty and national independence are not enough. Our liberty can lead to license and our independence to *godless arrogance*. We who are Christians understand that in addition to our political freedom the soul of man cries out for *spiritual* freedom.

A nation is no better than her people. The mere existence of a charter or a Constitution does not make us great. Just having a flag, an army, and a navy does not equal excellence.*Along with our political freedom we must be spiritually free, free from profane materialism, free from vulgar sensuality, free from childish and psychopathic racism, free from injustice, free from arrogance and contempt for the weak and powerless.

The Bible says, "Righteousness exalteth a nation and sin is a reproach to any people" (Proverbs 14:34). Nation after nation has crumbled in the dust of history and has been blown away by the winds of time. Old Pharaoh and the Egypt of Amenhotep passed away with *its* glory and splendor; the Assyria of Sennacharib is buried in the desert; the Babylon of Nebuchadnezzar and Belshazzar has long since fallen; the Persia of Darius and Xerxes was supplanted by Greece and Rome; and they were supplanted by Spain and England. Kingdoms come and go. Dynasties rise and fall. And if America would be truly great, if her destiny is to be fully attained, she must be a nation under God.

From the earliest of days in America, Baptists set themselves apart and made it plain that the civil government was one thing and the church another. And while the civil government controlled a part of the common life, the church sought to bring about a spiritual transformation in the hearts of men. The civil government sought freedom from taxes, soldiers, and navigation laws. We in the church sought freedom from sin and the devil, emancipation from hate and pride, freedom from racism, tribalism, and dead religion. This verse in Galatians says it all, "Stand fast in the liberty wherewith *Christ* hath made us free. . . ." And remember, "If the Son makes you free, you will be free indeed" (John 8:36, RSV).

When Christ has set you free, for *one* thing, you are able to see worth and dignity in all of God's children, from the least to the greatest. Paul said that we should not be bound by our old inherited prejudices and sins, but we should be transformed by the renewing of our minds. And if the mind is in us that was in Christ, we will see *worth* and *dignity in* all God's children. Christ saw worth in a slick tax collector like Zacchaeus; he saw worth in a woman being stoned for adultery; and he saw worth in a penitent thief on the cross.

If Christ has set you free, you will see worth in little children whose parents have neglected them; you'll see worth in the aged and the sick who never made much money and who ought not to be embarrassed to use food stamps or to live in fear of illness or live in dirt and filth; you'll see worth in those who have suffered poverty and isolation, who thought that crime and drugs were their answer, who are piled up in our jails and prisons, and who are waiting for us to learn a way of rehabilitation and to commit ourselves to it. If Christ has set you free, you'll know what he meant when he said, "When I was *hungry*, you gave me no *meat, thirsty,* you gave me no drink, *naked* and you wouldn't clothe me, a *stranger* and you wouldn't take me in, *sick* and in *prison* and you wouldn't visit me." When Christ sets us free, we see worth in the least of his little ones.

Next, when Christ has set you free, you want to see the quality of life improved in the nations and you want to see the society humanized. You see beyond your own economic and social class and your station in life and you want to see opportunity expanded so that everyone can maximize his or her potential. Jesus said, "I am come that ye might have life and have it more abundantly."

Some people have entered the race of life with some serious impediments. They began with illness, or in dire poverty, or in a moral climate that gave no promise of a decent life. But with some help they can come to their own fulfillment.

In 1968 I went to Africa with Vice-President Humphrey. We flew in Air Force One. It was a great and exciting trip for me.

When we reached Nairobi, I saw a tall black fellow with a heavy beard coming toward the plane. I recognized him. He had played football against our team ten years earlier. He waited and gave me a big hug. I thanked him for meeting me. But he said he didn't. He had come to meet the Sergeant, a huge Air Force sergeant, thundering down the ramp. They hugged tighter and longer. One of them was coaching at Nairobi's University College; the other was a security chief on Air Force One. Both had grown up just like brothers in a home for orphans in the East. Both grew up without their parents. With help, folk can make it. You see this when *Christ* has set you free!

When Christ has set you free, you want to tell everybody you know what a *blessing* you have found, what power *propels your* life, what joy fills *your* soul, and what peace possesses your mind. The Bible says, "If any one is in Christ, he is a new creation; the old has passed away, behold, the new has come" (2 Corinthians 5:17). You want to spread the good news. If *any* man! You want everybody to know about Jesus. This is not just a theory or an abstract idea; it is not just another religious fad—it is two thousand years old; it is not an emotional excursion or a psychological cop-out. It has borne the test of time. "He came unto his own and his own received him not. But as many as received him, to them he gave *power*—power *to become* the sons of God." (See John 1:11-12.)

The Baptists have always held as crucial this primary, authentic religious experience. Most people *know* about Baptist insistence on the separation of church and state; they *know* of Baptist belief in baptizing only believers, those who choose on their own volition to be disciples of Christ. And we Baptists have a *reason* for those beliefs. We don't believe that a duke or a baron, a queen or a king, a parliament or a state legislature can make a man or a woman a

"soldier of the cross,
a follower of the Lamb."

We don't believe that anyone *else* can vote *you* into the kingdom.

We believe that an infant can be prayed for, blessed, and dedicated to God, but no one has the power to initiate anyone else into the kingdom of God; for if you dwell in the kingdom, you have to *choose* to obey God's commandments, *plead* for the forgiveness of your *own* sins, and *experience* the indwelling of the Holy Spirit. You have to be *born* again, not of flesh and blood, but of the water and the Spirit.

So we cannot accept a state church, and we don't want the government controlling religion. We believe that we should render unto *Caesar* that which is *Caesar's* and unto *God* that which is *God's*.

We are citizens of two countries. We are citizens of the United States of America. And even though the nation is not perfect, it is our country. Her flag we honor, her praises we sing, and for her destiny we pray. But we are also citizens of the kingdom of God, from everlasting to everlasting, over which Jesus Christ is Lord of lords and King of kings.

Some years ago I was president of a college in Richmond, Virginia. I had two small sons. We had a highway that came through the campus. It was U.S. Highway #1. But it was also Lombardy Street in Richmond. Now, I always told my boys to be careful. I said, "When you step into that road, you are on Lombardy Street in Richmond and you are also on Highway #1. Don't forget that. If it was only

Lombardy Street, it wouldn't be so bad. You would only have to worry about the laundryman, the bakery truck, the neighbors, and the milkman. But it is more than Lombardy Street and some think it is only Highway #1. So, remember, when you stand on that single strip of concrete, you are standing both on Lombardy Street and Highway #1."

And so today, right now, right here, I am a citizen of the United States. I carry her passport, pay the taxes required, obey her laws, and celebrate her founding. But right now, in this place, I am also a child of the living God, a citizen of heaven, a member of the church of Christ, and a dweller in the kingdom of God.

So, I obey *another* set of laws; I follow *another* and a higher code of ethics; and I honor another leader, even Jesus, the Son of God. I became a citizen of the United States by being born of Velma and Herbert in Norfolk, Virginia, July 13, 1921. I am a citizen in that other kingdom because one day *the Lord* lifted me out of a horrible pit, set my feet on a rock, and put a new song in my mouth, and told me to go in peace and sin no more. And I'll tell everybody I know that ever since that wonderful day, my soul's been satisfied. "I looked at my hands and they looked new, I looked at my feet and they did too." And, "I have a *new name,* over in Zion. I have a new name!" My old sins have been drowned in a sea of forgetfulness, and my old account has been settled. I've been saved by the blood of Jesus and my salvation has been purchased by his death on Calvary's cruel cross, and I'm *happy.* I'm saved.

So, I live in the United States of America, and on her birthday I want to beat a drum and blow a bugle.

But I also live in the kingdom of God, and I want to celebrate that, too! Let everything that hath breath praise the Lord.

> Praise him for his mighty acts: praise him according to his excellent greatness.
> Praise him with the sound of the trumpet: praise him with the psaltery and harp.
> Praise him with the timbrel and dance. . . .
> Praise him upon the loud cymbals: praise him upon the high sounding cymbals.
> Let everything that hath breath praise the Lord.
> Praise ye the Lord.

—Psalm 150:2-6

This Is the Life

Leon C. Riddick

I am come that they might have life, and that they might have it more abundantly (John 10:10).

Most of us who call ourselves Christians, and claim to be living Christian lives, are merely inflated bodies, drifting with the godless winds of the age. Our only purpose for living seems to be the satisfying of our wants, our lusts of the flesh, and our insatiable hunger for pleasure.

A man who works five days a week, buys a little food and some liquor, that he might eat and drink over the weekend, relaxes in his easy chair and in a half-drunken stupor exclaims, "This is the life."

A youth who has no other purpose in life than to work hard that he might buy a fast car and live a fast life with the fast crowd in the dens and dives where he is robbed of physical energy and spiritual power declares, "This is the life."

Leon C. Riddick is a graduate of Shaw University. He has undertaken special study at Drew University and has been honored with the Doctor of Divinity degree by both Shaw and Virginia Union Seminary. Pastor of the Mt. Carmel Baptist Church of Charlotte, North Carolina, he is active in many civic, educational, and community organizations.

A young woman who has ignored the Christian way of life and has accepted the Hollywood formula for abundant living measures the values of life in terms of bust, hips, and makeup. And when this underfed, reduced, and thoughtless one can secure a job where she can display her jewels of flesh, the claim is, "This is the life."

Or, when we can move our glorified bodies into a split-level house and split our families because of our split personalities, boast of our unfaithfulness, and make a joke out of every law of common decency, the claim is, "This is the life."

Or, when we spend all our spare time chasing anything or everything that can give us a thrill, that produces pep, but robs us of spiritual power and the will to be representative sons of God on this earth, a voice thrilled by canned joy exclaims, "This is the life."

Then, when we feel weak and void of power, no longer do we lift our eyes unto the hills from whence cometh our help, but unto the medicine cabinet from whence cometh our tranquillizers. After we have swallowed a few pharmaceutical boosters, we relax and exclaim, "This is the life."

I wonder if this is the life of which Jesus spoke. Can life be lived, really lived, apart from some task, some duty, some obligation, some labor, that strengthens the soul and glorifies God? Is a man really living when he has no purpose in life other than to eat, drink, live in fine houses, wear fine clothes, die and be placed in a fine casket and buried in a fine grave plot?

I wonder if God's only purpose for creating us was that we might grow up and grow fat, die and become fertilizer for the earth, and cause the vegetation to grow more beautifully where our decaying carcasses lie. Could this be the only purpose for existence? Are we to conclude that the material things, the things we can see and touch, are all that matter? As for me, the spiritual gyroscope in my own soul, that keeps me in a vertical relationship with my Creator and a horizontal relationship with my fellowman, precludes any such positive answer. I have to say, "No."

Someone has said: "We live in deeds, not years, in thoughts, not breaths, in feelings, not in figures on a dial." Yet after a span of years on this earth, all many people have to show for their life is a birth certificate attesting that they came and a death certificate assuring that they went.

"I am come that they might have life, and that they might have it more abundantly."

A man's life cannot be enriched unless that man is God conscious. He may heap unto himself the riches of this world without ever possessing the riches of God. A man cannot enrich his life by suffering alone. The question is, "What is he suffering for?" We suffer for that which pleases us but will not suffer for the righteousness of God. Men are willing to suffer to perpetuate an ideological, sociological, limited, and provincial way of life, without ever asking themselves, "Is this God's way?" A man cannot enrich his life by constantly investing his spiritual and material resources in the nonessentials of this world. If a man would enrich his life, he must invest in divine necessities. Our businessmen must be told that in the divine economy the welfare of people takes priority over profit. Our politicians must be made to know that the welfare of the people takes priority over their selfish ambitions! Church leaders and officers must be made to know that a right relationship with God is more important than holding office.

No man can live the stewardship life; no man can enrich his spiritual life, unless he knows how and what to add to and subtract from his life and how to divide for the good of others. Man plus God has always equalled victory. Man plus God equals creative and purposeful living. We know how to add, but we have added the wrong digits and have gotten the wrong answers. We know how to add more gadgets to our homes and more power to our cars, but not more Christ to our lives. And we have come now to measure our spiritual lives in terms of material possessions. We have been deluded by the agents of hell into thinking that material success is a stamp of God's approval for our ways of living. A man may be successful according to the standards of the world and a failure according to the commands and demands of Christ. Abundant living is not merely successful living, but victorious living. A man may have success in the midst of evil, but no man can be victorious over evil without adding Christ to his life. Jesus didn't come that we might have success but that we might, through him, attain to victorious living.

A young man went to Jesus one day desiring to know how he might enrich his life. He wanted to know what good thing he could do to attain that quality of life called eternal. Here was a young man who was successful. He was rich and he was a ruler. That's success according to the thinking of carnally minded men. He had succeeded in adding to the stockpile of his material possession, but he didn't know how to subtract. He was rich in things, money, pride, and position, but spiritually bankrupt. There was a hunger in his soul that he had neglected. He lived for things and by things. What he possessed had eclipsed the Sun of righteousness and blotted from his view the Star of Bethlehem. Jesus said to him, "The spiritual poverty of your life is chronic, and in order for it to be enriched, you need an operation. You go and sell what you have, give to the poor, and come and follow me." When what one has begins to corrode his soul and makes it difficult for him to maintain the proper relationship with his God, it's time to sell out. When the perishable things in your life become more important than the unchanging God of your life, it's time to sell out. What did this successful young man do? He kept his fleeting success and his perishable riches, turned his back on Jesus, as if to say, "I don't believe you," and walked out into everlasting oblivion. This is the tragedy of it all. If ever we turn our backs on anybody, it's Jesus. Most of us sing a lie in churches when we say, "I'd rather have Jesus than silver or gold."

It is the set of a man's affection that enriches his life. No man who is a fool about the things of this world can ever have an enriched spiritual life. The apostle Paul wrote to the Christians at Colossae saying, "Seek those things which are above" (3:1). If human life is to be enriched, it must become identified with that which cannot be verified in a chemical laboratory. It must become a part of that which cannot be weighed on scales. Taking hold of the intangible and invisible possessions gives meaning to life and purpose to human existence. Such is the personal discovery of the reality of Christ. The heaven-inspired wisdom of the soul causes one to know that he has found the pearl of great price and is willing to let go all that perishes that he may obtain the imperishable.

When one's affection is set on things of this world, he is a go-getter, but when his affection is set on things above, on the eternal verities of God, he becomes a "go-giver." Victims of spiritual poverty are go-getters but not "go-givers."

Abundant living is that quality of life that enables us to go the second mile. Most of us "faint in the day of adversity," on the first mile. We never reach the second mile that Christ talked about. We have a tendency to conform to the ungodly environment about us, and conformers can never be transformers. We do not come into abundant life on the first mile, but we must go the second mile. It is on the second mile that we discover true spiritual values. It is the second mile that strengthens the spiritual constitution of the soul. It is on the second mile that we learn how to leap the barriers of racial hatreds and hell-inspired prejudices. It's on the second mile that we meet the companion who is a burden bearer and one whose yoke is easy and whose burden is light. It is on the second mile that we experience the "mysterious reserves of life"—that when material things have fled, sickness hangs a drapery of darkness about us, and friends question our integrity, we can still worship at the altar within our own life with these words, "The Lord gave and the Lord has taken away; blessed be the name of the Lord."

A shared life enriches life. This is the life—a shared life. No man discovers the true values of life until he shares this life. We don't really learn how to share until we learn how to turn loose. Every man who inhales the fresh air of God's world must exhale or die. A man is dead when he fails to exhale. We cannot continue to inhale the blessings of God without exhaling. We must share. Spiritual death is just as certain as physical death when we fail to exhale spiritually. This was the trouble with the rich man of whom the Bible speaks. He had inhaled of great riches, fine clothes, and good food, but he failed to exhale on Lazarus. His soul withered. He died, and in hell he lifted up his eyes.

We serve a God who shared. There was no need for God to be absolute and eternal goodness all by himself. There were men of earth who were infested with all that was evil and opposed to good. Therefore, God so loved the world that he shared. He caused to become flesh a portion of himself, and heaven announced that his name should be called Jesus. Yes, God shared—God so loved, and so shared, that whosoever believes, even now, in God's way of sharing, shall discover a quality of life that shall not perish.

We are reluctant to share because we are afraid of losing what we have. Jesus our Savior has taught us that the best way to have is to let go. But we don't understand this strange paradox. It does not fit into the scheme of thinking of the twentieth century. And so, we are afraid. But I've got good news for you. He who invests his life in the service of God, and in creative and redemptive goodwill, invests in the gilt-edged securities of heaven, and the market has never been known to fluctuate. He invests in a spiritual bank where the assets always exceed the liabilities. If you are afraid of losing your life, I've got good news for you. The empty tomb is heaven's guarantee that you'll find it. Yes, I've got good news for you. Share your life, because eye has not seen, neither has ear heard, nor has it been revealed all that the Lord God Almighty has in store for you. This is the life.

I am a bit disturbed about all the fuss we are making over integration. The Lord knows that I hate racial segregation and discrimination. I want to see every human being on earth enjoy all the rights and privileges that are his. But, I think that we have lost sight of something. We seem to think that if we can get an integrated school system all over the U.S.A., and integration in neighborhoods and apartment houses, and integration in all the hotels, restaurants, and public carriers of human cargo, that this will be the life. This is mere spatial integration. It is not enough to have spatial integration, we need an integration of the spirit. We must be careful lest we fall into this trap of hell—the improvement of man and society. It is not enough that man be improved, but man must be born again. When education has finished with the improvement of man, the preacher must tell him about regeneration. God is not satisfied with merely an improved society; he wants a reborn society. It is not enough that we be made-over creatures, but we should be new creations. Integration can never make men Christians, but regeneration will make men to become sons of God and followers of the Christ. We seem to think that, if a man can be in a spatially integrated society, he will become a new creature. It is not so. But, "If any man be in Christ, he is [not shall be, but is] a new creature; old things are [not shall be, but are] passed away; behold, all things are [not shall be, but are] become new." (See 2 Corinthians 5:17.) This is the life.

We are accountable to God for this life. We are not our own, for we have been bought with a price. God did not give us life that we might drift aimlessly through a span of years, die, and leave behind us as monuments superhighways, beautiful golf greens, jet planes and handmade satellites. When we come to the end of our earthly sojourn and must stand before the throne of the judge of all the earth, we will hear him say, "Give an account of your stewardship! What have you done with your life?" I don't want to have to tell him about our guided missiles and misguided men.

I don't want to have to tell him about my academic achievements and laurels that men of earth heaped upon me.

I want to be able to tell him that I used my life to lift up the Christ and to guide somebody to the Christian way of life.

I want to be able to tell him that I lifted somebody who had fallen, comforted somebody who was sad, fed somebody the bread of life, guided some wayward sheep back to the fold, and was a friend to somebody who was friendless.

I want to be enough like Christ to give a positive accounting of my stewardship. I don't want to stand before my God with a boweddown head and say, "I have played the fool."

What kind of accounting did Christ give of his life? I believe that upon his return to his Father in glory, he could say:

You gave me a dark night on which to be born, and I turned it into eternal day. You gave me a stable into which to be born, and I consecrated it into a shrine forever. You gave me the dust of the earth, and I used it as a pharmaceutical plant, and created a salve that did open blind eyes. You gave me your word and devils had to flee, the sick were made well, the lame made to walk, and the dead to live again.

You gave me a well curb for a resting place, and I used it as a pulpit from which I preached a sermon that started the flow of an eternal fountain in a woman's life. Water broke out in dry places, and a whole country was evangelized therefrom.

You gave me a few unpromising men and I made them to become foundation stones in the kingdom of God, and penmen of words of eternal truth.

You gave me a seamless robe, and I used it to wrap born and unborn generations into your plan of salvation.

You gave me the Garden of Gethsemane as a resting ground, and I used it as a praying ground.

You gave me a cross, and I used it to break the enslaving chains of hell, bridge the chasm that separated man from God, and left words for oncoming generations saying, "If I, if I, be lifted up from the earth, I will draw all men unto myself."

You gave me a borrowed tomb into which to be buried, and I made it to become the gateway to eternal glory.

This is the life!!

Ain't No Difference
in the Fare

Edna L. Smith

How many times have I heard my dear old mother, in the backwoods of Alabama, remind her family, "Ain't no difference in the fare."

How many times have I wondered, over and over again, "What does she mean?" But now I have become a woman and have put aside my childish ways; now that I think like a woman, reason like a woman, act like a woman, I understand what my mother meant.

As the gospel writer, Mark, wrote: "He that believeth and is baptized shall be saved; but he that believeth not shall be damned" (Mark 16:16).

So now I know certain truths. One, *Belief* is our common lot. Two,

Edna L. Smith is a commissioned missionary and a licensed gospel preacher and teacher. An instructor at Chicago Baptist Institute, she teaches church history and sociology. Mrs. Smith has traveled abroad in Africa and Haiti, with the C.C. Adams Foreign Mission Bureau. As a professional nurse for twenty years, coupled with her ministry, Mrs. Smith is a preacher much in demand because of her extraordinary insight and care for the problems of the whole person.

She is a graduate of Malcolm *X*, Jr., College, Moody Bible Institute, and Governor State University.

Belief, successfully withstood, can be a means to spiritual blessing. Three, *Belief* can be successfully retained.

The question is raised loudly. How? How? The answer returns clearly: like Christ, we must meet certain conditions.

We must *know* the word of God. ("It is written.")

We must *believe* the word of God. ("It is written.")

We must *obey* the word of God. ("It is written.")

If we, like Christ in the wilderness, *know—believe—obey—*we too shall rise in triumph. Belief can be successfully retained, upon three conditions which *Christ* met—one, he believed in God; two, he knew God; three, he obeyed God. Christ here on this earth met three conditions and successfully retained his *power.* By doing so, other men became curious and wanted to have a talk with Christ. They wanted to be saved—but did not know how, or what to do.

Let me illustrate. There was a man of the Pharisees named Nicodemus, who was a ruler of the Jews. He was convinced that Christ was a teacher who came from God; and he knew that no man could perform the miracles that Christ had performed unless God was with him.

Nicodemus *believed* this. And he came to Christ by night for a personal interview. John 3:1-21 tells the story. He wanted to know how a man could be born again, when he is old. In other words, "Lord Jesus, how can I be saved?" Jesus answered, "Verily, verily, I say unto thee, except a man be born of water and of the spirit, he cannot enter into the kingdom of God. That which is born of the flesh is flesh; and that which is born of the spirit is spirit. Marvel not that I say unto thee, ye must be born again."

"The wind bloweth where it listeth, and thou hearest the sound thereof, but canst not tell whence it cometh, and whither it goeth: so is every one that is born of the Spirit." In other words, *belief* is the key to the kingdom and to being saved. *"It Ain't No Difference in the Fare."* "For God so loved the world, that he gave his only begotten Son, that whosoever believeth in him shall be saved."

There was another certain man which had an infirmity thirty and eight years, who waited by the pool in Jerusalem. An angel went down at a certain time into the pool and troubled the water. Whoever, then, after the troubling of the water, first stepped in was made whole of whatever disease he had.

Jesus was there for a feast of the Jews, and he saw the man lying by the pool. He knew that this man had been in that condition for a long time, and he said to him, "Wilt thou be made whole?"

The crippled man answered him, "Sir, I have no man, when the water is troubled, to put me into the pool: but while I am coming, another steppeth down before me."

Jesus said to him, "Rise, take up thy bed, and walk." Immediately the man was made whole, and he took up his bed and walked. (See John 5:1-9.)

This man who believed in Jesus had withstood the pressures of life for thirty-eight long years. No doubt he suffered much because of his infirmity. But because he knew Jesus Christ, and believed in him, he was healed. When Jesus Christ spoke to him, he obeyed and received a spiritual blessing as well as a physical healing of the body. It is written that he was "made *whole*." He paid his fare through belief. My friends, there "ain't no difference in the fare." We all must believe that Jesus is the Son of the living God.

For it is written that when Jesus was being crucified, there were two thieves crucified with him, one on the right hand, and another on the left. Many people reviled him and did not believe that *He* was the king of Israel, nor did they believe that he was the Son of God, because he did not come down from the cross and save himself. It is written, "One of the malefactors which were hanged railed on him, saying, If thou be Christ, save thyself and us. But the other answering rebuked him, saying, Dost not thou fear God, seeing thou art in the same condemnation? . . . for we receive the due reward of our deeds: but this man hath done nothing amiss. And he said unto Jesus, Lord, remember me when thou comest into thy kingdom. And Jesus said unto him, Verily I say unto thee, Today shalt thou be with me in paradise. . . . And when Jesus had cried with a loud voice, he said, Father, into thy hands I commend my spirit: and having said thus, he gave up the ghost" (Luke 23:39-43, 46).

The second malefactor believed in Jesus and received his spiritual blessing directly from Jesus. According to Luke 23:43, this malefactor had common belief; he successfully retained it and received his blessing even after his crucifixion. I tell you, "It ain't no difference in the fare." Whosoever believes on the Lord Jesus Christ shall be saved.

Belief is the fare to the kingdom. We all have to pay that same fare to board that heavenly bound train. Jesus paid his fare, and so will we have to pay our fare. It may seem hard, but God has and will grant us a certain amount of power to overcome the obstacles on this earth— that we may believe and receive our reward in his kingdom, because, friends, "It ain't no difference in the fare."

When we arrive at the depot, the train will either be there or approaching soon. The sign will read, "Heaven Bound." Christ is the conductor; you will have to purchase your ticket in advance. Because when you step on board, he will call out, "Tickets, please!" (No money—only the ticket). No ticket, no ride! "It ain't no difference in the fare." Are you paying your fare? Or maybe you have already purchased your ticket. If you have—OK. If you have not, then make a down payment today. Just sign on the dotted line . . . . Lord, I believe, and I want to be saved. Thank you, Jesus. He saved me, and I know that he will save you, if you only believe. Be determined! Be like the song writer; make your start today:

Lord, I have started to walk in the light
Shining upon me from heaven so bright;
I bade the world and its follies adieu,
I've started in, Jesus, and I'm going through.
I'm going thro', yes, I'm going thro';
I'll pay the price, whatever others do;
I'll take the way with the Lord's despised few,
I'm going thro', Jesus, I'm going thro'.[1]

Dedicated to my mother, Roxie L. Sanders, Birmingham, Alabama. From my mother's favorite song, and my mother used the phrase oftentimes, "AIN'T NO DIFFERENCE IN THE FARE."

---

[1] Herbert Buffum, "I'm Going Through, Jesus."

Inquiry into
the Night

Kelly Miller Smith

(A Christmas Sermon)

... Watchman, what of the night? Watchman, what of the night? The watchman said, The morning cometh, and also the night: if ye will inquire, inquire ye: return, come (Isaiah 21:11-12).

Those who still have the grace to wonder whether or not they dare hope raise a persistent question as they see themselves enveloped in the thick darkness of the present. The question which rushes to their lips from their aching hearts is this: "Watchman, what of the night? Watchman, what of the night?"

The gaily colored lights which adorn our Christmas trees and our

Kelly Miller Smith is a well-known American Baptist and Progressive Baptist preacher, lecturer, scholar, and pastor. At an early age he pastored Mt. Heroden Church of Vicksburg, Mississippi. He is a graduate of Morehouse College and Howard University. Dr. Smith was a close associate to the late Dr. Martin Luther King, Jr., and also a civil rights activist. Presently he is the Assistant Dean of Vanderbilt University's Divinity School, and pastor of First Baptist Church, Capitol Hill, Nashville, Tennessee.

homes do not give even the illusion of day. Ours is an inquiry into the night! The music of Christmas which fills the air does not mute the cry nor drown out its persistence. The superficiality of our customary observance of Christmas is but a cruel hoax to those who look to it for hope and help. The raucous "ho-ho-ho's" of the street corner Santas must give way to the cries of misery heard in a multitude of ways in our streets today. The night that we now know is not quite silent and its holiness escapes us. Our midnights are not quite so clear as those about which we sing.

The prophet Isaiah characterized the Edomites' suffering oppression at the hands of the Babylonians as crying out to the watchman on the wall: "What of the future? Dare we hope? Watchman, what of the night?"

And so, at Christmastime, we express our concerns. All tinsel aside, let us, for the moment, forget about the seasonal things we do to cover up our emptiness and our heart hungers. Let us forget about the gifts we make to conceal our guilt and to camouflage our contribution to the brokenness of the human family. Let us shove aside the "cheer" we conjure up to hide our tears. Let us peer beyond the decorations on our windows which keep us from really seeing our brothers. Let us come to grips with truth. The truth is that we are in one ungodly, unholy mess. Graphic descriptions of the times in which we live are not necessary. We know what these times are like. The tensions and anxieties are felt on both sides of the tracks. As some have put it, there is a hollowness at the center of life in our nation. Regardless of how we spell our names or how we keep our hair or whether our grammar is chaste or broken or what our address is, we know that we are enveloped in the experience of night. The questions are these: What do we have to look forward to? We know that it is night, but how much longer? Will it ever let up? Are we doomed to eternal darkness with the bitter unresolved problems that so beset us? Watchman, what of the night? Watchman, what of the night?

Watchman

When this question is raised, we all look around as if to say, "I know the question is not directed to me. I wonder who the watchman is." Who has the answer? Who can impart the life-giving information that can save us? The truth is that we are not lacking in answer men.

All about us they are volunteering an answer to the query.

From the vantage points of their various disciplines the answers are coming.

Some are impressed with our technological prowess and suggest that we turn in this direction to find out where we truly are. We have moved to the distant moon with comparative ease. Surely technology can direct us as we inquire into the night. We recognize our technological advancement as obedience to the divine command that we subdue the earth. There is something of a divine fulfillment in this work and we must not see this as in opposition to God's requirement for man. Yet, we must acknowledge that technology unsupported by certain other considerations and resources cannot point the way. It can provide only a partial answer to the query "What of the night?" It does help us to see our way, but in a limited sense. We must go further.

With the militarism that characterizes so much of our world, there would be those who would feel that military might can be the actual determinative. The ultimate answer is seen by many of our generation to be in violence, in armed might. How tragic it is that some can see the force of violence as the only social corrective! For some, the only response to social frustration is armed might. The agencies of violence are seen as the proper determiners of our course and of our destiny. Obviously, the power of armed might cannot serve as our watchman. We cannot expect the shedding of blood to be the way to herald the dawn. Rather, violence can plunge us into a darkness blacker than a thousand midnights. When we raise the pertinent question "Watchman, what of the night?", we do not address the question to those whose god is militarism.

Then, there are the political determinists who believe that the answer is to be found in the political arena. For them the political situation is the indication of where we are and what the status of the night is. The only thing that matters, they would insist, is who is in office. There is no question but that to a great extent our destiny is tied in with what happens politically and it is important to participate in the political process in an informed and creative way. But this alone is not enough. Much is left to be desired if we only turn to the political arena and ask the question, "Watchman, what of the night?"

Those of us who are professionally in the field of religion and others as well do not hesitate to say that the problems which beset us are spiritual problems and that we can find our way only when we realize this singular fact. I once saw a magnificent building in Rome called the Pantheon. It is said to have been erected well over two thousand years ago by Agrippa. It is called the Pantheon because it was supposed to provide space for representations of all of the gods being worshiped in Rome. When the question came as to how to represent the God of Abraham, Moses, and Jacob, it was decided that the roof would be left open so that the sunlight could flow in and cover all of the other "gods" there. This is what we of the church must say: We do not disparage what is being done in other areas, for we know that much of this is the work of God. It is, indeed, our task to find out where God is at work in the world and to join him there. The true watchmen are those who have a peculiar spiritual sensitivity which will allow them to see the hand of God in the technological process and to know that he is not to be held aloof from the political arena and who know that the issues which confront us are spiritual issues and that our direction is spiritually determined!

It is to those who have this kind of sensitivity that we turn and raise our anguished cry: "Watchman, what of the night? Watchman, what of the night?"

The Morning Cometh . . . and Also the Night!

Perhaps the intentionally ambiguous answer which the questioner receives in our Scripture passage is an appropriate one for us: "The morning cometh, and also the night!"

The real message of Christmas is simply this: The morning comes. Perhaps, only with lingering footsteps, but it does come! The battered, beaten, tossed, and driven Israelites held on to a hope. They held on to a messianic outlook. Deep in the heart of their faith was the insistence that God had not deserted them nor left them with only the deep shadows of night. The stars of hope shone in the night. The dream did not die, and with the music that filled the air of the little town of Bethlehem came the unmistakable message: "The morning cometh."

Night is the time when babes cry and when the sick toss and turn upon their beds of pain and cry out, "I would to God it were morning." Night is the time when vices come out of their hiding places and boldly stalk the streets. It is the time when danger is greatest. But hearken to the unmuffled cry of a babe in Bethlehem. Look, there is a light upon the mountain! And soon the light which appears upon the mountain will penetrate the deep darkness of the valleys and illumine our pathways. Yes, "the morning cometh."

Recently, I was on the campus of a large state university which is known for anything but its spiritual concerns. Yet, there stood a young man with a long beard, a sweat shirt, and blue jeans. On the jeans was written the word "Jesus," and he held a Bible in his hands. A little farther along was a booth where a young man and a young woman were talking, of all things, about religion and about Jesus Christ. The dean of the chapel at Kalamazoo College has commented that the basic quest among college youth is a spiritual quest. There is a light upon the mountains. We are again beginning to ask the right questions and with this, "the morning cometh."

The other part of the answer is this sobering announcement ". . . and also the night." Slaves escaping from Egypt's flesh pots had to face the gaping waters of the Red Sea. Bethlehem cannot be properly considered without Calvary. There is Palm Sunday, but there is also Good Friday. There is light, but there is darkness. The morning light is breaking; the darkness disappears. But the morning sun must move on into afternoon and fade in the evening. Then the shades of evening will appear once more. And night will fall.

Human nature is just that way. Jesus Christ comes as the light of the world, and that is what Christmas is all about. Yet, we will see the light and walk in darkness. We will know where the high roads are, but still walk in the low places. The light is available, but because of our disobedience, our willful defiance of God, we walk in darkness. God provides us with the light. We choose the darkness.

So we go on with our shedding of human blood and our dehumanization process and our poisonous venom of hatred. So we go on closing our eyes to the wretched of the earth and stopping our ears to the cries of the hungry. So we go on with our jitters and nervous disorders and our psychological sicknesses. You see, God has created us for certain specific purposes; and when we fail to live in accordance with those purposes, we break ourselves down. If Christmas says anything to us at all, it should call us back home. It should call us from darkness to light. It should say to us that we need not live our lives in darkness. There is a light available. However simplistic it may sound, Jesus IS the light of the world. He is the Lord of life. He speaks creatively to the issues which confront us if we but have ears to hear.

It is not a mistaken cry that the morning cometh. It does indeed come. God has seen to that. The people that sat in darkness have seen a great light. God has come through again. There is light upon the mountain. Through him, the morning comes. Yet, partly because of the persistent waywardness of man, the night also comes. There are advances and reversals. All of the darkness is not brought on by man's waywardness. There are still unresolved mysteries in this area. There are still problems which beset us which remind us of the fact that God is still in charge and is not confined to the puny powers of man.

The light is there, but also the darkness. The morning cometh, but also the night.

Inquire Ye, Return Ye, Come

The prophet suggests that the stance of the questioner should be maintained. Those who raise sincere questions have not given up hope. They face the light and the darkness, and they do not give up. They see that there is a certain integrity involved in the question mark. Man ought to raise some questions at times. We should not disparage those who raise questions in sincerity. In this manner we learn. Someone has said that man is a "question-asking, answer-seeking animal." This is a part of being man. We have a right to inquire into the darkness which surrounds us. We have the right to look around us for the right watchman to whom the question is to be addressed. When we see our bright mornings change into dull afternoons and dark evenings, we should not give up, but raise some more questions, or raise the same questions afresh.

During this turbulent time the questioners come—even after Christmastime. They are bright youth and snow-crowned aged, and they are asking, "Watchman, what of the night?"

There are the poor who have seen more nights than days, more misery than comfort, and they cry out through parched lips, "Watchman, what of the night? Watchman, what of the night?" There are the young who are confused by our ambivalence and uncertain values and they want to see a change; so, in their own way they ask, "What of the night?"

These questions will continue to come. Little children will ask them of their parents. They will come to the educational institutions. They will come in the barbershops and the pool halls and in the places of work, on the job: "What of the night?" And, yes, we who call ourselves the church will have to give an account of our stewardship, sometimes to a strange and unexpected questioner, as he looks us straight in the eye and asks, "Watchman, what of the night?"

We must rummage back through the pages of history until we find again a straw-filled manger in a small town called Bethlehem. We must capture the light that filled and surrounded that manger. We must go over the hills and through the valleys of this life, holding on to the unfailing hand of him who was—and is—the light of the world.

How far has the night gone, watchman? How far has the night gone?

The morning is not far off, there is light in the sky; but there is more to endure, and it is always darkest before the dawn.

Nobody Like Him

Woodrow W. Taylor

What is thy beloved more than another beloved, O thou fairest among women? . . . My beloved is white and ruddy, the chiefest among ten thousand. . . . His mouth is most sweet: yea, he is altogether lovely (Solomon's Song 5:9, 10, 16).

The text comes to us from Solomon's Song. To me, this is the book of the Bible that is filled with romance. In this book there is a true love story. This book has been severely criticized by the skeptics and infidels who have tried to discredit the whole canon of the Scriptures because of its contents.

Even though there is difficulty in both the translation and the interpretation of this passage, it is generally agreed that it pictures or prefigures the courtship that existed between Christ and the believer, between Christ and his church. Christianity is a romantic venture.

Woodrow W. Taylor is Midwest President of the Progressive National Baptist Convention and National Vice-President of the Progressive Convention.

Since 1953 he has been the pastor of Shiloah Baptist Church, Chicago. He is author of several articles and sermons, among them "Sparks of God's Anvil."

There is thrilling romance in the experience of personal salvation. When the soul is united to Christ in love and devotion, a courtship is begun that extends throughout the life of the believer and Christ becomes nearer and dearer as the days go by. This courtship never becomes old and stale, but it is ever refreshing, and "every day with Jesus is sweeter than the day before."

In the picture before us we see a young woman who is desperately in love. It is a love which is both bold and daring. Her lover has withdrawn himself and she has become lonely. She longs for his presence. She seeks diligently for him. She is not satisfied even at the banquet table because her lover is not there. Her friends tried to make her happy, but all attempts in this direction were in vain. She tells her own story. "I left them because I was seeking him." What was true in her case is true also in ours. It is either "Him" or "them." If you prefer Him, you will be giving up "them." Those who prefer "them" are not worthy of Him.

Her friends, taking note of this peculiar love and loyalty which should characterize every Christian, were amazed and disturbed. This interest which was so profound, so reckless in its nature, caused them to seek for the secret of this love. They inquired for an explanation, which is recorded in the text: "What is thy beloved more than another beloved?" Why is it that you are not happy with us? Why is it that, in spite of the presence of your friends, you are still lonely? We seek to cheer and comfort you. We planned a banquet for you, and you left us at the table and went out into the streets. What is it about him that is so different from others? What is it that completely possesses you? Why is he so highly esteemed, so fascinating that he has every ounce of your devotion? The text also includes her reply, which is finally condensed into the words of the sermon subject: "Nobody Like Him."

This story is our pattern for loyalty to Christ, and it also obligates us to explain our loyalty by giving a reason for the hope that is in us. We must manifest our Christian devotion so as to convince the world that we have discovered a glorious reality in serving God. They must see in it a joy that the world cannot give nor take away. We can never explain fully the reasons for our attachment to Christ; we can say without any hesitation and without fear of contradiction: "Nobody like him." Certainly our knowledge is too limited to discuss fully the subject that deals with the Christ of God, but we can give a few points that will point to his superior greatness.

Nobody like him in his preexistence. He existed before time and before place. He existed in the bosom of the Father behind the purple curtain of eternity before the foundation of the world. The life of the Christ did not begin in the manger, and it didn't end on the cross. He always has been and always will be. Christ speaks of his preexistence in the intercessory prayer. He asks his Father to glorify him with the glory he had before the world was. The apostle John writes of his preexistence in the first chapter of his Gospel. He calls him the "Word." This Word was in the beginning. The "Word" was God. This "Word" created all things.

Christ, in speaking to the Jews, declares his preexistence when he tells them he was seen by their father Abraham in his day. He tells them that his presence goes further back than Abraham's past: "Before Abraham was, I am."

Nobody like him in his incarnation and birth. His incarnation defies finite comprehension. He was God wrapped in human flesh. In his flesh he was both God and man. He was no dwarf God or midget God, for we are told by the apostle Paul in his epistle to the Colossians that "in him dwelleth all the fulness of the Godhead bodily" (2:9). He who was the ancient of days became the infant in days. We must not stagger at this fact in unbelief. None of us can understand this mystery. His mother, Mary, his earthly father, Joseph, were both baffled at this mystery. While we cannot understand it, we must believe it. As one great theologian says, if one would stumble over the idea of the incarnation, he must stumble at the idea of creation, for God only reversed the order. God took a motherless woman from the body of a man in creation and took a fatherless man from the body of a woman in redemption.

In his birth, heaven hung out its brightest star and led the wise men from the East to Jerusalem. Heaven sent the angel-preacher and angelic choir to the Judean hills and broke the news to those shepherds who were watching their flocks by night.

Nobody like him in his person. He is the God-man, two natures in one personality. He protected the interest of heaven with his divinity and looked after our interest with his humanity. In his divinity, he is God's way to man; in his humanity, he is man's way to God—two natures harmonized but never blended. His divinity was never humanized and his humanity was never deified. As man, he went to the marriage in Cana of Galilee as an invited guest; and as God, at the marriage he turned water to wine. As man, he got on the ship and went to sleep; but as God, he calmed the raging sea. As man, he wept at the grave of Lazarus; but as God, he raised Lazarus from the dead.

Nobody like him in his works. His works gave witness to his divinity. He placed his works before his enemies as the star witness. Even when John the Baptist sent his disciples to Christ to make an inquiry as to his person, again Christ pointed to his work. He told them to "tell John the blind see, the lame walk, the dumb speak, the deaf hear, the lepers are cleansed, the dead are raised, and the poor have the gospel preached to them."

Nobody like him as a preacher and teacher. The record is: "He taught them as one having authority and not as the scribes." His hostile opponents had to testify: "Never a man spake like this man." The religious informer of the Jews said to him as the official spokesman of the great religious body: "Master, we know, thou art a teacher come from God. . . ."

If there are further doubts concerning this matchless person, I refer you to the Sermon on the Mount. There was no particular aid to worship, no choir, no devotional committee, no prayer meeting as a forerunner to the message, no pulpit nor rostrum; yet the message is still sounding down the corridors of time: "Blessed are the poor in spirit. . . . Blessed are the pure in heart. . . . Blessed are the meek. . . . Blessed are the peacemakers."

Nobody like him as a paradox. As judge of the quick and the dead, he was judged of sinful men; as creator of all things, he had nowhere to lay his head. He is our living water; yet he was thirsty. He was weary; yet he is our rest. He was physically unattractive; yet he is sweeter than honey and altogether lovely. He is King of kings; yet he is our constant companion.

Nobody like him in his suffering and death. Nobody suffered like him. He was born with the cross on his heart. If you think one can match his suffering, "Go to the garden, sinner; see those precious drops that flow, the heavy load He bore for thee, for thee He lies so low."

Nobody died like him. See him as he hangs on the cruel cross. I think the centurion's testimony will suffice in this case: "Truly this was the Son of God."

Nobody like him in his resurrection. He died. He was buried. The tomb was sealed with the Roman seal. The tomb was well guarded with soldiers; but there was a greater power on the inside than there was on the outside, for

> Up from the grave He arose,
> With a mighty triumph over His foes;
> He arose a Victor from the dark domain,
> And He lives forever with His saints to reign,
> He arose, He arose, Hallelujah, Christ arose. [1]

Nobody like him as a tried friend and constant companion. He was and he is. He is both the historic and the contemporary Christ. He was theirs and he is ours.

> In sorrow He's my comfort,
> In trouble He's my stay,
> He tells me ev'ry care on Him to roll;
> He's the "Lily of the Valley, the Bright and Morning Star,"
> He's the fairest of ten thousand to my soul. [2]

"Nobody Like Him!"

[1] Robert Lowry, "Christ Arose," Copyright 1916 by Mary Runyan Lowry, in *Hymns and Sacred Songs* (Hope Publishing Company), p. 244.
[2] Traditional, "I Have Found a Friend in Jesus."

The Greatest Proof

Morris Harrison Tynes

God so loved the world that he gave his only begotten Son, that whosoever believeth in him should not perish, but have everlasting life (John 3:16).

Widespread cynicism has led to a general quest for creedal certainty and a rational basis for religious hope. There is even an insistent demand for empirical proof that "God so loved the world that he gave his only begotten Son, that whosoever believeth in him should not perish, but have everlasting life." Our national mood indicates that not many fervently believe that God has demonstrated his love for us, "in that, while we were yet sinners, Christ died for us" (Romans 5:8).

Why do we not see the logic in life? All is ultimately balanced! Without pain we could not appreciate pleasure; without sorrow we could not appreciate joy; without despair—hope; without darkness—

Morris Harrison Tynes graduated from North Carolina A & T State University and pursued further study at the University of Michigan. He completed theological studies at Yale University. He is currently pastor of the Greater Mt. Moriah Baptist Church in Chicago, Illinois, and also consultant to the Department of Human Resources of the City of Chicago.

---

light; without error—truth; without hate—love; and without life temporal we could not appreciate life eternal. The contrasting dualities balance each other—man and woman, earth and sky, daytime and nighttime, time and eternity, here and hereafter. God has never given a hunger without providing a corresponding satisfaction. Our very thirst for water tells us that there are cooling springs somewhere. This utterance from the lips of the psalmist expresses both thirst and quenching, desire and discovery, quest and affirmation: "As the hart panteth after the water brooks, so panteth my soul after thee, O God!" (Psalm 42:1).

The test of any hypothesis involves the establishment of conditions consistent with the hypothesis in order to produce results predicted by it on the assumption that it is true. Among the necessary elements are meeting specified conditions, producing predictable results, and thereby validating the basic assumption. The first two conditions are generally accepted without argument, but the final element is a more subtle point that frequently escapes recognition as an important factor in the test of any hypothesis.

To illustrate: when ships were built of wood because it was commonly believed that in order to float they had to be built of materials lighter than water, the suggestion was made that ships could be built of iron and still float. A certain blacksmith argued that ships built of iron would not float, and he proved his point by tossing a horseshoe into a tub of water.

The blacksmith's belief that the hypothesis was untrue prevented the possibility of him formulating an experiment consistent with the hypothesis which could have produced the result predicted by it. If he had believed that the hypothesis was true, he could have tossed an iron washbasin into the tub of water instead of an iron horseshoe.

Leo Tolstoy asserted that there are two methods of human activity; and according to which of these methods people follow, there are basically two types of people. Some use their reason to discover the difference between good and evil and govern themselves accordingly. The others do as they wish and then use their reason to prove that what they did was right and what they did not do was wrong. The uselessness of attempting to alter by logic and debate attitudes rooted in emotional needs is classically illustrated by Gordon Allport in his book, *The Nature of Prejudice.*

A paranoid woman had the fixed delusion that she was a dead person. The doctor tried what he thought was a conclusive logical demonstration to her of her error. He asked her, "Do dead people bleed?" "No," she answered. "Well, if I pricked your finger, would you bleed?" "No," answered the woman, "I wouldn't bleed; I'm dead." "Let's see," said the doctor, and pricked her finger. When the patient saw the drop of blood appearing she remarked in surprise, "Oh, so dead people *do* bleed, don't they."[1]

Many persons do not really seek the truth. They seek proof or validation of their preconceived or prejudicial assumptions. The individual, for example, who possesses racial prejudice does not seek to subject his prejudice to the light of scientific truth. He seeks, instead, to justify his prejudice on the basis of limited, distorted facts. If he wants to prove that a certain racial group is dirty and shiftless, he will seek out such elements in that group to prove his point and thus reinforce the bias that reflects emotional inadequacies within himself.

Real proof involves an unbiased, objective evaluation of all available facts. However, some facts go beyond the province of scientific testing or validation. The authenticity of Christ can only be validated in the light of reason and human experience. Christ was either good or evil; responsible or irresponsible. If he was evil, he could not have gone about "doing good." If he was wholly good, he could do no evil! If he was responsible, he could not have lived irresponsibly.

Either his life and death make sense, or he was the craziest man who ever lived. And, if crazy or deranged, how could he have given us the profound wisdom of the Sermon on the Mount? From whence came the "authority" of his speech and the mighty power of his miracles? From whence came the brilliant insight of his youthful mind (at the age of twelve) sitting among the scholars in the temple? From whence came the mastery of his fasting, the majesty of his baptism, the mystery of his transfiguration, and the sublime heroism and dignity of his death?

It is quite human to want proof in matters of faith and belief. The devil wanted proof in the wilderness. "If thou be the Son of God, command that these stones be made bread" (Matthew 4:3). Thomas wanted proof in the upper room. "Except I shall see in his hands the

[1] Gordon W. Allport, *The Nature of Prejudice* (New York: Doubleday & Company, Inc., Anchor Books, 1958), p. 395.

print of the nails, and put my finger into the print of the nails, and thrust my hand into his side, I will not believe" (John 20:25). We want proof in domestic affairs, and we want proof in foreign affairs. To the Soviet Union we say, "We want concrete proof that you will honor and abide by a meaningful strategic arms limitation agreement." We want proof in social affairs of true friendship. A couple under the canopy of moonlit skies want proof of true love. Many children in the home yearn for positive proof of parental love.

A bitter, frustrated John in prison cries out for proof: "Art thou he that should come? or look we for another?" (Luke 7:20 and Matthew 11:3). Jesus, in effect, charged John's disciples to go back and tell him what they had seen and heard. Tell him that scales have been lifted from blinded eyes! Tell him that the lame have thrown their crutches away! Tell him that the lepers have been cleansed and restored to respectability! Tell him that the deaf have been made to hear! Tell him that the dead have been made to rise and walk out of graveyards! Tell him that the good news has been preached to the poor! And if this isn't enough proof for John, tell him that I have the power to summon twelve legions of angels and even convert these surrounding stones into microphonic witnesses that will testify to the glory of God's Son. (See Luke 19:40.)

The very "heavens declare" and prove "the glory of God, and the firmament sheweth his handywork" (Psalm 19:1). Hence, the universe is a magnificent evidence of the creative power of God.

If the world had created itself, then in it would be embodied all of the marvelous attributes of a Creator and thus we would be forced to conclude that the universe itself is God. However, no one has disproven the hypothesis that NO MATERIAL OBJECT CAN CREATE ITSELF. A design must have a designer!

The very first verse of the Bible proclaims that God was "in the beginning" of this world. To affirm that God was in the beginning is not to deny that he existed before the beginning. God has neither beginning nor ending; he is the eternal "I AM!" He is the ONE ETERNAL NOW! He is the "Alpha and Omega" of the ever-widening circle of infinite love. The universe itself is the handiwork and offspring of omnipotent love (Isaiah 40:1f.). For "God is love; and he that dwelleth in love dwelleth in God, and God in him" (1 John 4:16).

The Bible is a magnificent evidence of the wisdom and love of God. Jesus Christ is the highest expression and the greatest and profoundest proof of the existence of God. Without him, there would have been no need for the Bible. For the Bible springs from the prediction, anticipation, and actualization of his coming. Prophecy declared, "For unto us a child is born, unto us a son is given: and the government shall be upon his shoulder; and his name shall be called Wonderful, Counseller, The mighty God, The everlasting Father, The Prince of Peace!" (Isaiah 9:6). Anticipation responded, "And this shall be a sign unto you; Ye shall find the babe wrapped in swaddling clothes, lying in a manger" (Luke 2:12). Actualization concluded, "In the beginning was the Word, and the Word was with God, and the Word was God. The same was in the beginning with God. All things were made by him; and without him was not any thing made that was made. In him was life; and the life was the light of men. . . . AND THE WORD WAS MADE FLESH, AND DWELT AMONG US, (and we beheld his glory, the glory as of the only begotten of the Father,) full of grace and truth" (John 1:1-4, 14, emphasis added).

Four simple but historic items capture my imagination as symbolic proofs of God's love. A STAR! A MANGER! A CROSS! AN EMPTY TOMB! The star is not the reality! The star is but an impressive signature on the promissory note of redemption. The manger is not the reality! The reality is the concern of God which makes it possible. The cross is not the reality! The reality is the redemptive love of God which places it on a lonely hilltop!

The cross is a bloody romance between heaven and earth! The cross is a human mirror of God's divine love! The cross is heaven's medicine for earth's chronic sickness! The cross is heaven's remedy and pardon for earth's confusion and sin! The cross is heaven's absolution for earth's guilt! The cross is heaven's joy for earth's sorrow! The cross is heaven's hope for earth's despair! The cross is heaven's triumph for earth's disaster! But the cross is not the ultimate reality! The cross is but an historical symbol of God's eternal involvement in the sins and griefs of man!

The empty tomb is not the reality! The reality is the power of God that makes possible the empty tomb! The reality is the power of God that took the sting out of death and robbed the grave of its victory! The empty tomb is a joyous and triumphant sequel to the prophetic juxtaposition of the manger and the cross. The manger, the cross, and the empty tomb collaboratively affirm and authenticate "THE WORD BECOME FLESH" under the spotlight of a Bethlehem star!

The name—Jesus Christ—"is the dome of all vocal grandeur" . . . "a name which is above every name." And "neither is there salvation in any other; for there is no other name given among men, whereby we must be saved" (Acts 4:12). Jesus Christ is "THE WORD BECOME FLESH!" He is the "only begotten Son" who most concretely and personally expresses God's love for a lost and sinful world.

No unusual occurrences attended the births of Buddha, Brahma, or Mohammed! Nor were there any special dispensations with the coming of Plato, Aristotle, Socrates, or Confucius. But, WHEN THE WORD CAME, heaven hung its brightest star in the Bethlehem sky to mark the place where a Babe, ages older than his own mother, bent the datelines of history around an unpretentious stall! WHEN THE WORD CAME, the Grand Conductor of life's greatest symphony raised his majestic baton and directed the angels to sing "Glory to God in the highest, and on earth peace among men with whom he is pleased!" (Luke 2:14, RSV). WHEN THE WORD CAME, shepherds left their timorous flocks and wise men left their metaphysical kingdoms! WHEN THE WORD CAME, Herod got uneasy and the Roman Empire shook from stem to stern! WHEN THE WORD CAME, the Holy Spirit enlisted the service of a dove at the Jordan River.

WHEN THE WORD CAME, angry winds and raging seas timidly curled up in the arms of God! WHEN THE WORD CAME, a multitude was fed on five loaves and two small fish! WHEN THE WORD CAME, the unconscious water looked into the face of God and blushed! WHEN THE WORD CAME, chains began to fall from bleeding ankles, and childhood and womanhood were lifted to a higher level of dignity! WHEN THE WORD CAME, mystics became poets, poets became hymn writers, and philosophers became theologians! WHEN THE WORD CAME, Raphael and Michelangelo stole colors from the rainbow, and anthems, hymns, and hallelujah choruses toppled majestically down the stairway of glory! WHEN THE WORD CAME, a dead man got up out of his grave! WHEN THE WORD CAME, the sun draped itself in stygian

darkness and the moon became convulsed with a celestial hemor-
rhage! WHEN THE WORD CAME, an earthquake shook the
Savior's tomb!

Civilizations rise and fall! Social, economic, and political systems
undergo change! Yes, even "THE GRASS WITHERETH, THE
FLOWER FADETH:

BUT THE WORD OF OUR GOD
SHALL STAND FOR EVER" (Isaiah 40:8).

Additional Worship Resources
Published by Judson Press

Best Black Sermons, William Philpot, ed. 1972. Sermons that emphasize black dignity and proclaim God's power. 0-8170-0533-1

Biblical Faith and the Black American, Latta R. Thomas. 1976. Calls upon black Americans to rediscover the liberating power of the biblical message. 0-8170-0718-0

Children's Time in Worship, Arline J. Ban. 1981. Practical ideas for involving children in corporate worship. Extensive resource section for pastors. 0-8170-0907-8

The Church in the Life of the Black Family, Wallace C. Smith. 1985. Creative ideas for a holistic program that focuses on needs in education, employment, housing, health care, and personal identity. 0-8170-1040-8

Contemporary Biblical Interpretation for Preaching, Ronald J. Allen. 1984. Uses critical exegesis in a simplified manner to develop fresh biblical interpretations for sermons. 0-8170-1002-5

Creative Programs for the Church Year, Malcolm G. Shotwell. 1986. Focuses on personalizing the gospel message with special plans for every season. 0-8170-1102-1

Cups of Light . . . and Other Illustrations, Clarence W. Cranford. 1988. Two-hundred illustrations for sermons and meditations. 0-8170-1142-0

Dedication Services for Every Occasion, Manfred Holck, Jr., compiler. 1984. Thirty-five services for just about any special celebration. 0-8170-1033-5

God Is Faithful, Julius Richard Scruggs. 1985. Practical interpretations of great Bible truths offer help for facing personal disappointments and solving problems of social injustice. 0-8170-1060-2

God's Transforming Spirit: Black Church Renewal, Preston R. Washington. 1988. Discusses important elements of church renewal—prayer discipline, dependence on the Holy Spirit for guidance, helping members grow in discipleship, and ministry to the community. 0-8170-1129-3

Interpreting God's Word in Black Preaching, Warren H. Stewart. 1984. Five-point study of the hermeneutical process for interpreting and communicating the Word so that it will be relevant to the congregation. 0-8170-1021-1

Listening on Sunday for Sharing on Monday, William D. Thompson. 1983. How the preacher and the listening congregation can become a dynamic partnership for spreading the message of God's healing power. 0-8170-1000-9

Litanies for All Occasions, Garth R. House. 1989. Scripture-inspired litanies that allow the pastor and congregation to join together in lifting up to God their praise, petitions, and thanks for blessings. 0-8170-1144-7

The Minister's Handbook, Orlando L. Tibbetts. 1986. Practical resources for worship services, special observances, and special occasions in members' lives. 0-8170-1088-2

The Ministry of Music in the Black Church, J. Wendell Mapson, Jr. 1984. Shows how music can enhance worship. 0-8170-1057-2

Outstanding Black Sermons, J. Alfred Smith, ed. 1976. 0-8170-0664-8

Outstanding Black Sermons, Volume 3, Milton Owens, Jr., ed. 1982. 0-8170-0973

Redemption in Black Theology, Olin P. Moyd. 1979. Examines redemption as reflected in black history and folk expressions. 0-8170-0806-3

Sermon on the Mount, Clarence Jordan. 1970. An interpretation of Christ's sermon that explores today's problems. 0-8170-0501-3

Sermons from the Black Pulpit, Samual D. Proctor and William D. Watley. 1984. Thirteen sermons that call for a renewed commitment to discipleship. 0-8170-1034-3

Sermons on Special Days—Preaching Through the Year in the Black Church, William D. Watley. 1987. Sixteen sermons for all celebrations of the Christian year. 0-8170-1089-0

"Somebody's Calling My Name," Wyatt Tee Walker. 1979. Detailed history of black sacred music and its relationship to social change. 0-8170-0980-9

The Star Book for Ministers, E. T. Hiscox. 1906. Contains forms and suggestions for every type of service in which a pastor is called upon to participate. 0-8170-0167-0

Steady in an Unsteady World, Stephen A. Odom, ed. 1986. Fourteen selections from the unpublished sermons of Leslie Weatherhead. Each brings a message of hope for people facing uncertain futures. 0-8170-1097-1

Telling the Story: Evangelism in Black Churches, James O. Stallings. 1988. Challenges black Christians to recapture the power of their rich evangelistic heritage. 0-8170-1124-2

Those Preachin' Women, Ella Pearson Mitchell, ed. 1985. Fourteen sermons by black women that call Christians to develop positive attitudes and to find their identities by oneness in God. 0-8170-1073-4

Those Preaching Women, Volume 2, Ella Pearson Mitchell, ed. 1988. More sermons by black women. 0-8170-1131-5

Vision of Hope: Sermons for Community Outreach, Benjamin Greene, Jr., ed. 1988. Action-oriented sermons that offer a fresh view of the church's mandate for ministry to hurting people. 0-8170-1150-1